Early praise for *Learn Game Programming with Ruby*

I wish I had this book, Gosu, and a time machine. Twelve-year-old me would have had such a blast!

➤ **Jason Clark**
  Software Engineer, New Relic

Learn Game Programming with Ruby not only teaches one the basics of making games, but builds a framework to jumpstart an interest in programming. Definitely a must-read for beginners.

➤ **Rudy R.**
  Student, Age 16

Learn Game Programming with Ruby is an excellent addition to any Ruby programmer's library. If you're ready to move on from Scratch, you're ready for this book!

➤ **Douglas Gray**

This book is great for people who are curious about learning Ruby for the first time or for programmers with a little experience. With endless possibilities, this book lets you have fun at your own pace, explaining every step along the way.

➤ **Marianne K.**
  Student, Age 15

Learn Game Programming with Ruby

Bring Your Ideas to Life with Gosu

Mark Sobkowicz

The Pragmatic Bookshelf

Dallas, Texas • Raleigh, North Carolina

Many of the designations used by manufacturers and sellers to distinguish their products are claimed as trademarks. Where those designations appear in this book, and The Pragmatic Programmers, LLC was aware of a trademark claim, the designations have been printed in initial capital letters or in all capitals. The Pragmatic Starter Kit, The Pragmatic Programmer, Pragmatic Programming, Pragmatic Bookshelf, PragProg and the linking g device are trademarks of The Pragmatic Programmers, LLC.

Every precaution was taken in the preparation of this book. However, the publisher assumes no responsibility for errors or omissions, or for damages that may result from the use of information (including program listings) contained herein.

Our Pragmatic courses, workshops, and other products can help you and your team create better software and have more fun. For more information, as well as the latest Pragmatic titles, please visit us at *https://pragprog.com*.

The team that produced this book includes:

Brian P. Hogan (editor)
Potomac Indexing, LLC (index)
Cathleen Small; Liz Welch (copyedit)
Dave Thomas (layout)
Janet Furlow (producer)
Ellie Callahan (support)

For international rights, please contact *rights@pragprog.com*.

Printed in the United States of America.
ISBN-13: 978-1-68050-073-8
Printed on acid-free paper.
Book version: P1.0—September 2015

Contents

Foreword

Unlike most web pages or "normal" computer applications, 2D games do not follow a strict set of rules. Every game is different; one might be played from a top-down perspective, another might scroll from left to right, and another might be a turn-based puzzle game with square or hexagonal tiles. Some games follow a story; others can be played with friends. As you can imagine, the code for each game will be just as unique as its gameplay. This lack of a common structure can be quite intimidating. How do you start building a city-planning game, a virtual football match, or any other kind of game?

This book guides you through the process of writing four very different games. The exercises in each chapter will show you how to extend each kind of game. You can mix and match parts from different chapters, or try to mimic features from your favorite video games in Ruby. Try to structure the code differently every once in a while. Eventually, you will be able to build games that are unlike any example shown in this book.

While these games are different, some tasks—such as reacting to keyboard input, displaying image files, or playing sound effects—are the same. This book uses a library called Gosu, which provides all of these basics on Windows, OS X, and other operating systems. Gosu is a media library, not a complete game development kit. For example, there is no Map class or any collision-detection logic in Gosu because it is hard to design—much less *use*—a library that suits *all* kinds of games at the same time. This lack of reusable components is a good thing, though. It means that this book is less about learning Gosu and more about constructing games using universal programming constructs such as objects, methods, loops, and arrays.

The Ruby language is a great candidate for this task. Working with objects feels natural in Ruby, and games are fantastic for learning object-oriented programming. If you look at the screen, you can usually see which objects and classes are involved in a game, making it straightforward to model them in code.

But Ruby is also very concise. Game design is about experimentation and refinement, not about having a master plan from the start. Building a game is often about deleting code and trying something else. In a verbose programming language, discarding code can be frustrating. Who wants to give screens full of painfully handwritten code? In Ruby, the same logic might fit into a few lines of code, and rewriting it is a breeze.

With these tools in your hands, enjoy inventing your very own games!

Julian Raschke
Gosu Developer

Acknowledgments

Before I thank anyone else, I want to thank my wife Michelle. Throughout the time I spent working on this book, she never said a word that wasn't supportive. This book is a testament to her patience and good nature, more than any other factors.

My students at Lincoln Sudbury Regional High School were my original inspiration to write this book, as many of them had questions that went beyond what we could cover in our short Introduction to Programming class. They showed me time and again that imagination and creativity are the secret sauce, that you don't have to be an expert to have a great time making games, and that beginners can make games that are exciting and fun to play. A shout-out to Chris A. and Mia F., who asked some of the hardest questions.

This book would not be possible without the work of Julian Raschke, who wrote the Gosu gem for Ruby. In addition to this gift to the Ruby community, he was patient and generous with me personally, reviewing the book and helping me understand some of the finer points of the library he wrote.

Thanks to my technical reviewers for their insightful suggestions and for finding my mistakes, both in the code and in its explanation. I am grateful for their expertise and time. Thank you to Craig Castelaz, Douglas Gray, Scott Hofmann, Marianne K., Steve Morss, Rudy R., Darian Springer, Charlie Stran, and Stephen Wolff.

I'd like to acknowledge my colleagues at Lincoln Sudbury Regional High School for creating a place where intellectual curiosity is nurtured and where risks and experimentation are encouraged and expected. May Lincoln Sudbury forever remain a "different kind of place."

And a final thanks for the patience and perseverance of Brian Hogan, my development editor; managing editor Susannah Pfalzer; and all the fine people working at the Pragmatic Programmers. I brought my idea to them because I love their books, and I thank them for the opportunity to work with them on this one.

CHAPTER 1

Introduction

Hello and welcome. This is a book about making games with and for your computer—games like some of the ones you love on your computer, your phone, or your game console. By working your way through this book, you'll make four games, each of a different type. You'll learn how to open a window on your computer screen and then fill it with moving pictures. You'll make those images interact with each other, and you'll control them with your computer's mouse and keys.

The games we make will feel pretty familiar to you. They aren't copies of other games, but they do use familiar patterns and principles that you'll be able to use to make your own games. The techniques you'll learn for making a spaceship fly around by pressing keys on the keyboard can also help you move a chicken across a road full of traffic. Each chapter in this book is based on a few different elements of game creation, and each element is applicable to a wide range of games.

The goal of this book is to help you bring your own ideas to life. When you've learned these elements of game development, you'll be able to take a game you've imagined and create that game so that it runs on your computer—and also on your friends' computers.

Ruby and Gosu

Along the way, you'll level up your programming skills. Becoming a better programmer will help you make great games, and making games will help you improve your programming skills. To make the games in this book you'll use the Ruby programming language, along with a game library called Gosu. Ruby is a great language both for learning to program and for making games.

It has "an elegant syntax that is natural to read and easy to write."[1] The Ruby language focuses on *objects*, and this makes it a great fit for creating games, as you'll see as you work through this book.

The Gosu game library will provide the structure for your games, while leaving their design and content completely up to you. It gives you the tools you need to place images on the screen, move them around, and play sounds to spice up your game. At the same time, it doesn't do anything you won't understand. You and your code will always be in control of what's happening in your game window. Gosu is also a great springboard to other platforms. In particular, working with SpriteKit, Apple's framework for making two-dimensional games for iOS and OS X, feels like a natural step up from writing games with Gosu.

Ruby and Gosu are free, open source software that work well on both Windows and Mac OS X computers. You can download everything you need, so it's easy to get started, and perhaps you'll find other people willing to learn game programming along with you in your school or town. There is an online community dedicated to game programming with Ruby and Gosu, with a showcase where people share their games and a forum where they ask and answer questions.[2] Many people in this community have shared both finished games and the *code* for those games, and these can be great sources for learning and inspiration.

What You'll Need

First, you'll need a computer. It can be a Mac running OS X 10.9 or later, or it can be a Windows computer running Windows 7 or later. You need to be comfortable with the file system on your computer, so you can save files where you want them and organize them into folders.

To get the most out of this book, you'll need a little programming experience. If you have already used Ruby, you're ready to go. If you have experience with a different programming language, you might want to pick up a book such as *Learn to Program [Pin09]* or *Programming Ruby 1.9 & 2.0 [FH13]* and learn a little Ruby syntax before you start on the games in this book.

The Road Ahead

As you go through this book, we'll be making some games together. The games follow a progression, and each chapter assumes that you have worked through

---

1.   https://www.ruby-lang.org/en/
2.   http://www.libgosu.org/

the preceding chapters. Here is a summary of what you'll be learning in each chapter.

- In Chapter 2, *Get Ready*, on page 5, you'll set up your computer to use Ruby and Gosu to write games.

- In Chapter 3, *Creating Your First Game*, on page 15, you'll make a simple game. You'll learn how a Gosu game is organized and how to use Gosu to open a window on your computer, fill it with pictures, and move those pictures around.

- In Chapter 4, *Creating a Sprite-Based Game*, on page 39, you'll begin a new game, Sector Five, in which a player controls a spaceship that shoots down enemy invaders. Each thing you draw on the screen will be a *sprite*, and you'll learn to create a class for each type of sprite in the game.

- In Chapter 5, *Managing Lots of Sprites*, on page 57, you'll learn how to manage many sprites by organizing them with arrays. By iterating through these arrays, you'll be able to handle the movement and interactions of many sprites in the window at once.

- In Chapter 6, *Adding Scenes and Sounds*, on page 79, you'll break your game into multiple scenes, giving it a start scene with some instructions and an end scene with credits. You'll learn how to add music and sound effects to finish Sector Five.

- In Chapter 7, *Creating a Puzzle Game*, on page 101, you'll create a puzzle game called Twelve. This game focuses on user interaction, and you'll learn how to write code to implement the rules of the game.

- In Chapter 8, *Making a Platformer Game with Physics*, on page 125, you'll use a physics engine to make objects move naturally. In Escape, a hero will jump between platforms, dodging boulders that fall, spin, and bounce.

- In Chapter 9, *Making a Side-Scrolling Game*, on page 157, you'll learn how to make your platformer game scroll, using a camera object to follow the hero's motion. This will allow you to have a game field that is bigger than your screen.

- In Chapter 10, *Package and Share Your Game*, on page 173, you'll learn to package up a game into a single executable so you can share it with your friends.

When we're finished, you'll have a better understanding of how games are put together, as well as some new programming tools in your toolbox. You'll be ready to take your own ideas and turn them into games.

Bumps in the Road

Whether you're following a tutorial or writing your own code, it can be frustrating when things don't work. This book tries to anticipate some of these situations and give you some strategies to deal with them. At these places in the tutorial, you'll find a section with some ideas for how to solve particular problems.

What If It Doesn't Work?

We'll explore different sorts of problems that can occur and look at ways to solve them. You'll learn how to interpret some common errors and look at ways to find answers on the Internet.

Writing games is fun, and hopefully the rewards of making your programs work will outweigh the frustration you feel when they don't. Sometimes the answer will come to you only after you've walked away from the computer for a little while. Stick with it! Persistence is one of the most important assets a programmer can have.

What's Next

Before you can actually start making games, you'll need to install a few things on your computer. The next chapter will explain what you need and will take you step by step through getting ready.

CHAPTER 2

Get Ready

Using the Ruby programming language and the Gosu game library, we'll create some amazing games with images, sounds, and Ruby code. But before we can start writing those games, we need to install a few things on the computer. To write programs, we'll need to use programs! Some of those programs will be the kind you might be used to—programs you launch by clicking an icon. Others do their work in the background; they are unseen libraries of code that your computer needs to run the programs you write. All together, the tools and programs you use to write your games are called your *development environment*. The environment you need to make games with Ruby and Gosu consists of the following elements.

Ruby

Ruby is the programming language we'll use to create our games. If you've written Ruby code before, great! If you haven't, the tutorials in this book are complete, and you can learn some Ruby by following them. To get a deeper understanding of Ruby, you might want to take a look at a book like *Learn to Program [Pin09]* or use an online tutorial, such as the one on Code Academy.[1]

Developer Tools

To run Ruby programs that create windows on the screen and play sounds, we need to install some background libraries. These libraries let our Ruby programs access the system resources needed to run our games.

Gosu

Gosu is the library we'll be using to write our games. Gosu is a collection of Ruby classes designed to make writing games simple and fun.

---

1. http://www.codecademy.com

A Text Editor

We'll use a text editor to write our programs. A text editor creates plain text files, without any formatting. Microsoft Word and Apple Pages are not text editors, because the files they produce contain all sorts of information in addition to the text in the document. You can use any text editor to write code, but some have useful features, both for writing programs and for running them right from the editor.

How you install these items depends on which operating system you're using. If your computer runs Windows, read on. If you're using a Mac, skip ahead now to *Getting Ready with OS X*, on page 9.

Getting Ready with Windows

With Windows, you start by installing Ruby. Point your browser to http://rubyinstaller.org and click the big red Downloads button. This will take you to a page with a list of items, as shown in the following image.

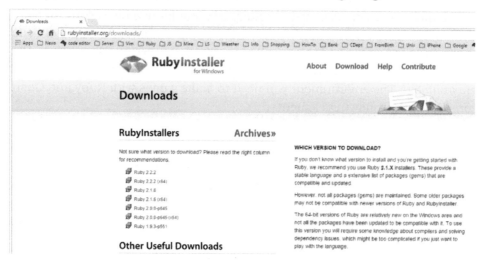

You install both Ruby and the Developer Tools from this page. From the list of Ruby installers, choose the one for Ruby 2.2.2 (or 2.2.x, where x is a number larger than 2). Don't get the one labeled (x64).[2]

---

2. The goal of this book is to make installing Ruby and Gosu as simple as possible for a wide range of users and computers. When this was written, the newest version of Ruby available on Windows was Ruby 2.2.2. When you do the installation, that might no longer be true. Look for the version that starts with 2.2. If you already have a version of Ruby, or if you want to use the latest and greatest, by all means give it a try. For a setup that will get you writing games as soon as possible, use these instructions for Ruby 2.2. All the games in this book work with any Ruby version of 1.9.3 or later.

When you run the installer, you are first asked to accept the license. Then a dialog box, shown in the following figure, presents you with three check boxes. Check the two shown and continue.

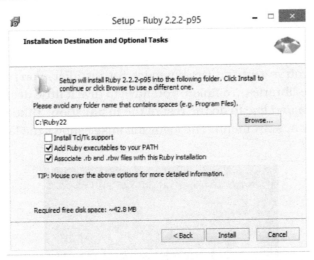

The installer creates a folder Ruby22 in the C:\ directory and puts your version of Ruby in that folder. You can use the File Explorer to see that it's there.

From the same web page, a little further down, download the Development Kit that is "For use with Ruby 2.0 and above (32bits version only)," as shown in the following image.

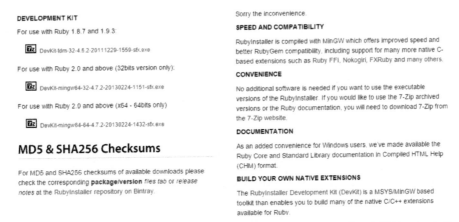

When this download is finished, run the installer. You need to tell the installer where to put the Development Kit. Put it in a folder of its own, called DevKit, alongside the Ruby22 Folder. To do this, enter C:\DevKit in the window, as shown in the following image.

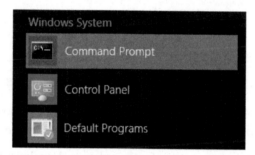

Even though you've run the Development Kit installer, you're not finished installing these libraries. To finish, you have to dive a little deeper. You need to use the *command line* to do the rest of the installation. Take a look in your launch window or start menu. The following image shows the launch window in Windows 8.

Find and open the Command Prompt application. This application opens a window on your screen with a prompt where you can type commands to the computer. When you've completed a command and hit the Enter key, your computer will respond with the results of your command. When you open the Command Prompt, your location in the file system is your home directory. To finish installing the Developer Kit, move the location where commands are executed into the new DevKit folder. Type cd \DevKit at the command line and press the Enter key.

```
C:\> cd \DevKit
C:\DevKit\>
```

The prompt at the command line now indicates that you're ready to execute commands in the DevKit folder. The next command finds the Ruby you installed previously and sets up the Development Kit to work with this Ruby. Note that you're running a Ruby program called dk.rb with this command.

```
C:\DevKit> ruby dk.rb init
[INFO] found RubyInstaller v2.2.2 at C:/Ruby22

Initialization complete! Please review and modify the
auto-generated 'config.yml' file to ensure it contains
the root directories to all of the installed Rubies you
want enhanced by the DevKit.
```

This is good news, since the Development Kit is going to enhance Ruby 2.2 just as you want it to. You don't need to do anything to the config.yml file. Next, at the command line, run the following.

```
C:\DevKit> ruby dk.rb install
[INFO] Installing 'C:/Ruby22/lib/ruby/site_ruby/devkit.rb'
```

Your Ruby is ready. You can now execute Ruby programs, either from the command line or directly from a text editor, which we'll look at soon. You still need to install Gosu, which you'll also do from the command line. Gosu is a Ruby gem, meaning a package of code that extends what Ruby can do. The Gosu gem includes code that opens a window on your computer screen, fills it with images that move, and plays sounds through your speakers. At the prompt, type gem install gosu and then sit back; the installation may take a while.

```
C:\DevKit> gem install gosu
Fetching: gosu-0.9.2-x86-mingw32.gem (100%)
Successfully installed gosu-0.9.2-x86-mingw32
1 gem installed
```

Gosu is now ready. The last game in the book uses one more gem, called Chipmunk, which is a physics library and will help handle some complicated math. Install Chipmunk now by typing gem install chipmunk at the command line.

```
C:\DevKit> gem install chipmunk
Fetching: chipmunk-6.1.3.4.gem (100%)
Temporarily enhancing PATH to include DevKit...
Building native extensions.  This could take a while...
Successfully installed chipmunk-6.1.3.4
1 gem installed
```

You are now ready to write some games. Skip the section on installing for OS X and move on to *Install a Text Editor*, on page 13. If something went wrong, you should instead read *What If It Doesn't Work?*, on page 13.

Getting Ready with OS X

These instructions have been tested on OS X Mavericks (10.9.5) and on OS X Yosemite (10.10.3). There was a bug in OS X 10.9.2 and earlier that required a complicated workaround, so check the OS X version you're using.

To do this installation, you need to be logged in to the computer with an account that has administrator privileges. If you're working on your own computer and yours is the only account, you're all set. If not, you can see what privileges an account has in the Users and Groups panel of System Preferences.

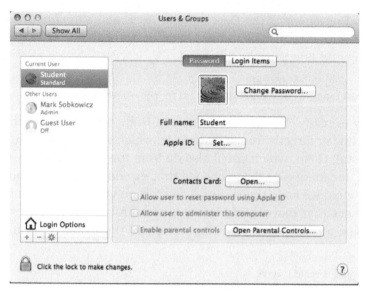

If you're logged in on an account that says Standard instead of Admin, you should get some help from the owner of the computer, either to change your account to an admin account or to help you do the installation on the owner's account. You won't need to be an administrator to write and run programs, just to install the software in this chapter.

All the steps of this installation are done using the *command line*. Find and run the application called Terminal. It's in a folder called Utilities in the Applications folder. Terminal provides a prompt where you can type commands. The prompt is a $ symbol. When you're typing the commands in this chapter, don't type in the $.

On OS X, Ruby is already installed. You can make sure of this by typing the following at the command line:

```
$ ruby --version
ruby 2.0.0p481 (2014-05-08 revision 45883) [universal.x86_64-darwin14]
```

The Ruby version that comes with OS X is version 2.0.0. The number following the "p" is a build number. There are newer versions of Ruby, but this version is fine to get started writing some games. Your Ruby is ready.

Next, install the command-line tools. Xcode is Apple's all-in-one programming environment, and the development tools you need are a small part of this large package. Apple provides a way to install just the parts you need by typing the following at the command-line prompt:

```
$ xcode-select --install
```

When you press Return after typing the command, a window will open and ask if you'd like to install the tools now, as shown in the following figure.

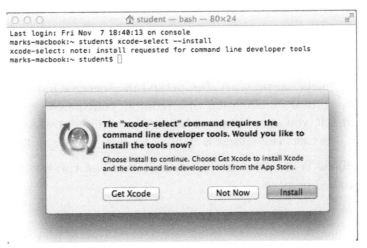

Choose Install and wait a few minutes as the tools are installed.

The next thing you'll install is called Homebrew. Homebrew is a package manager for the Mac, which means it's used to install and update other software. You're going to use it to install three libraries of code that Gosu needs but that don't come with the Xcode Command Line Tools. To install Homebrew, type a single long line of code at the command-line prompt and then press Return. You can copy and paste it from the Homebrew website, at http://brew.sh. The install instructions are near the bottom of the page.

If you prefer, you can type the following command on a single line in Terminal:

```
$ ruby -e "$(curl -fsSL
    https://raw.githubusercontent.com/Homebrew/install/master/install)"
```

This line of code first downloads the Homebrew installer, which is a Ruby program. It then runs the installer with the ruby command. The installer shows you exactly what it is installing as it goes. It asks for your password to run the installation.

```
WARNING: Improper use of the sudo command could lead to data loss or the
deletion of important system files.  Please double-check your typing when
using sudo.  Type "man sudo" for more information.

To proceed, enter your password, or type Ctrl-C to abort.

Password:
```

This warning might sound scary, but behind the scenes it's doing the same thing as any software installation that requires your password. When you use sudo yourself, you should indeed be very careful about what commands you give. In this case, Homebrew is using it for you, and it's quite safe.

Once Homebrew is installed, it recommends that you run brew doctor to see that it's installed properly.

```
$ brew doctor
```

Homebrew might have some recommendations for you, or it might just reply that everything is fine, with the note, "Your system is ready to brew."

You can now use Homebrew to install some libraries. The three libraries you'll need are sdl2, libogg, and libvorbis. They enable Gosu to play a variety of audio formats, and you won't be able to install Gosu without them. Install them using Homebrew by typing the following at the command line:

```
$ brew install sdl2 libogg libvorbis
```

Homebrew provides a series of messages as it downloads each item and installs, or *pours*, it.

Once these are installed, you're finished with Homebrew, but not with the command line. Next, you'll install Gosu itself. Gosu is a Ruby gem, or package, and to install it you'll use the sudo command. Because you're typing it yourself this time, type sudo gem install gosu very carefully at the command-line prompt. You may need to provide your password again.

```
$ sudo gem install gosu
Fetching: gosu-0.9.2.gem (100%)
Building native extensions.  This could take a while...
Successfully installed gosu-0.9.2
```

The last game in the book uses one more gem, called Chipmunk, which is a physics library that handles some complicated math. Install Chipmunk now at the command line:

```
$ sudo gem install chipmunk
```

The messages you get will be almost the same as the ones you got when installing the Gosu gem. You're now ready to write some games with Gosu. To actually write them, you'll use a text editor, which we'll discuss in *Install a Text Editor*, on page 13.

What If It Doesn't Work?

Following directions like the ones in this chapter can be difficult. Typing commands at the command line is tough, because every character has to be exactly correct. Even if you follow every direction in this chapter, something might not work. You might be using an older system, or a different Ruby version might already be installed on your computer. If the command line says there is an error, scroll back and see whether you typed the command exactly as given. If you didn't, start again at that point. If you can't figure out where the install started to go wrong, start at the beginning. The installers we've used will not cause any problems if run more than once. If you are still having trouble getting Ruby and Gosu up and running, there are some more discussions of how to set up Gosu on the Gosu Wiki. [3] The Gosu website also has an issues page where Gosu users post problems they are having, including installation problems. [4] In addition, you can use the forum at the Pragmatic Programmers dedicated to this book to talk with other readers, as well as with the author.

Install a Text Editor

You can write Ruby programs in any text editor, such as Notepad on Windows or TextEdit on OS X. Your experience will be much better with a specialized programming text editor, which can help you by automatically indenting code, coloring your code based on its syntax, and more. If you have a favorite and know how to use it, by all means use what you have. If you don't yet have a programming editor, using Sublime Text 3 is a great option for working with Ruby and Gosu.

Sublime Text 3 is a cross-platform text editor with versions for Mac, Windows, and Linux. You can download the most recent version of Sublime Text 3 at http://www.sublimetext.com/3. When you are editing a Ruby file in Sublime Text, you can run it with Ctrl-B on Windows or Command-B on OS X. This is a great convenience compared to running it each time from the command line.

---

3. https://github.com/gosu/gosu/wiki
4. https://github.com/gosu/gosu/issues

You can try a full-featured version of Sublime Text 3 for free and use it to do the tutorials in this book.

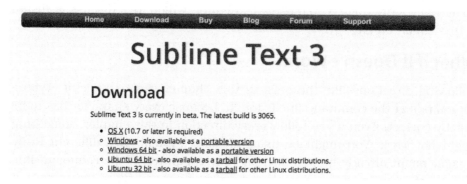

Organize Your Workspace

Each game you write consists of a number of computer files. Some are text files you create with your text editor. Others are image and sound files you make with other software or find on the Internet. To keep these files organized, make a new folder on your desktop and name it Games. For each game you make, put a new folder inside this one. In addition, make some folders to store images and sounds you make or find that you might want to use in a future game.

Then get the source code and other files for the projects in this book. They've been compressed and archived into a single file that you can download from the web page for this book, https://www.pragprog.com/book/msgpkids. Download that file and unarchive it. Move the resulting folder into your Games folder and take a look inside. Inside is a folder for each of the games we're going to make. Each game folder has several folders inside. The one with the name ending in _starter has just the image and sound files for the game. The others are versions of the game at different points along the path to completion. You can use them to check your code if you get stuck or as starting points if you want to focus on a particular part of the book.

What's Next

You're ready to start! You have Ruby along with the Gosu and Chipmunk gems installed and ready to go. Next, you'll create your first game with some Ruby code, the Gosu library, and a few images.

CHAPTER 3

Creating Your First Game

In this book, we're going to use Ruby and Gosu to make a variety of games. Our first one, Whack-A-Ruby, will be a pretty simple game in the spirit of Whack-A-Mole. When the game is started, a window opens on the screen, and an image of a ruby bounces around the window, blinking on and off. Players try to hit the ruby with a hammer while it's visible, scoring points when they succeed. The finished game will look like this.

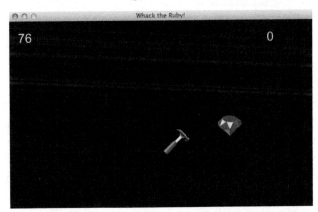

We'll create this game step by step, typing code into the text editor and running it. Along the way, you'll become familiar with the most important classes and methods in the Gosu library, and you'll learn how they work together to provide the framework for your games. When you're finished, you'll be able to:

- Make a window appear on your computer screen.
- Draw an image in the window.
- Move the image around.
- Detect mouse clicks.
- Display text on the window.

We're ready to start. Fire up your text editor—it's time to write some code.

Make an Empty Window

Each game you'll write starts by opening a window on your screen. That window is where you'll bring your games to life, drawing images and making them move. Gosu provides you with a *class* for drawing that window, called Gosu::Window. This class does more than just draw the window; it also provides *methods* that give structure to your games. Each time you write a game, you'll start by creating a *subclass* of Gosu::Window. For your first game, that subclass will be called WhackARuby.

To create this class, make a new folder called WhackARuby, inside the Games folder you made in *Organize Your Workspace*, on page 14. Using your text editor, make a new file and save it in that folder with the name whack_a_ruby.rb.

To use its classes in your project, you'll need to include Gosu with require. The empty WhackARuby class looks like this.

`WhackARuby/WhackARuby_1/whack_a_ruby.rb`
```
require 'gosu'

class WhackARuby < Gosu::Window
end
```

You can run this code, but nothing will happen yet. You need to add a *method* to your class to tell Gosu a few things about your window, and you need to create and run an *instance* of your game.

The first method you'll add to your new class is called initialize(). This method is run when you create an instance of your class, so in your game it will be run only once. In the initialize() method of WhackARuby, you'll tell Gosu what size window you want. Your window will be 800 pixels wide and 600 pixels tall. Pixels are the unit of measurement for everything in Gosu. You can make your windows bigger than this, but an 800×600-pixel window will fit on any modern computer screen with some room to spare, so it's a good size to use if you'd like to share your games with friends. Inside your initialize() method, you'll call the super() method and pass in the dimensions of your window. This sends your dimensions to the initialize() method of Gosu::Window.

You'll also set the window caption in the initialize() method. You can give the player some simple instructions—"Whack the Ruby!"—at the top of the window.

After your class code, you'll create a single instance of your game and call its show() method. You didn't write the show() method—it's part of Gosu. Your whole file now looks like this.

WhackARuby/WhackARuby_1/whack_a_ruby.rb

```ruby
require 'gosu'

class WhackARuby < Gosu::Window
  def initialize
    super(800, 600)
    self.caption = 'Whack the Ruby!'
  end
end

window = WhackARuby.new
window.show
```

(handwritten annotations: "instance of class is created", "runs when an", "window", "dimensions of window", "window caption", "part of gosu")

Run the program, using either the editor or the command line. If you're using Sublime Text, you can run your code with Ctrl-B on Windows or Command-B on OS X. If you're using the command line to run your program, navigate to your game folder and then use the ruby command.

```
$ ruby whack_a_ruby.rb
```

However you run the program, an empty window will appear. Try changing the window to 1000 pixels wide. Try changing the caption. Each time, run the program and see the results. Then change it back, so you can keep following these instructions. You should get used to running your program often. It's much easier to find any mistakes you might have made after typing a few small changes than after making a whole bunch of changes in different places in the file.

Regardless of how you configure the size of your window, it's still empty and black. So let's look at how you draw images inside it.

But first, this is probably a good time to look at the programmer's perennial problem: my code doesn't work.

What If It Doesn't Work?

You've followed the tutorial, typed a bunch of code, and then run the game. You expect the window to appear, but it doesn't. What happened? How can you fix it as quickly as possible and get back on track?

When you run your game, either with a text editor or with the command line, the program generates *output*. This program output can be very informative when your program isn't working properly. You won't see the output while the game is running. You'll only see it when the game is over or when it quits unexpectedly.

There are three ways a Ruby program can fail to work. We'll explore all three in more depth at various points in this book. The way the program fails tells you something about the cause, and knowing something about the cause can help you fix the problem and get back to making your game.

Your game doesn't run at all.   Ruby can't understand your code, and you have a *syntax error*. It is structured incorrectly in some way. One common problem is that you left off an end statement. Read the program output for hints.

Your game runs, but it crashes at some point.   You might see a window for just a fraction of a second, or the game might crash at some point while you're playing. One cause of this is that you spelled a method name incorrectly or spelled a variable name differently in two places. In this case, you can also read the program output to see whether that helps you figure out the problem.

Your game runs, but it doesn't behave as you expected. Problems like this can be both frustrating and fun to solve. They are like puzzles, and later in the book we'll explore some ways to dive in and see what's going wrong.

Let's look at some program output. The following output was generated by leaving the end off the initialize() method.

```
/Users/mark/Desktop/WhackARuby/whack_a_ruby.rb:10: syntax error,
unexpected end-of-input, expecting keyword_end
window.show
          ^
[Finished in 0.1s with exit code 1]
```

In this case, Ruby tells us that the error is a syntax error and that Ruby reached the end of the file but was expecting an end statement. The error isn't on line 10, though, and putting the end after window.show doesn't fix the problem. With a missing end statement, Ruby tells you what the problem is, but you have to find the spot yourself.

Here is an example of a misspelled method. In this case, window.show is replaced with window.shoe.

```
/Users/mark/Desktop/WhackARuby/whack_a_ruby.rb:10: in `<main>':
undefined method `shoe' for #<WhackARuby:0x007fc7f1049780@__swigtype__="
_p_Gosu__Window"> (NoMethodError)
[Finished in 1.3s with exit code 1]
```

The error message has some confusing parts, but the meaning is clear. We have an "undefined method shoe."

Whether you're following a tutorial or creating your own game, *run your program as often as possible*. This is the best thing you can do to make finding errors easier, since the error is likely in the code you just wrote.

Getting Images for Your Games

When you think about your favorite video games, what do you see in your mind? Whether you're thinking of *Angry Birds*, *Mario Kart*, or *Pac-Man*, you're probably thinking of the memorable art in the game. Your games will need art, and so do the games in this book.

Maybe you're an artist, or you know one who wants to make art for your games. If so, great! But if not, don't despair. There is plenty of art online, and much of it is free for you to use in your games. There is a list of some excellent sources in *Images and Sounds*, on page 181, and you'll find much more if you search the Internet.

The art for Whack-A-Ruby comes from the website http://www.openclipart.org. The images of a ruby and a hammer are in PNG format, which works well with Gosu on both Windows and OS X. You can find these files in the source code you downloaded in *Organize Your Workspace*, on page 14. Here is what the images look like:

The website makes it clear that all of their art is in the public domain and may be used for "unlimited commercial use." I encourage you to pay attention to the licenses under which art is released. Not everything on the Internet is free for you to use in your games, but plenty is. Some artists allow use of their art but require that you give them credit, also called *attribution*. Others require that if you use their art in your game, you have to give your game away under the same license they used to release their art. And others let you use their art with no strings attached. If you want to make your own art, go for it! Export it from your drawing program in PNG, GIF, or JPEG format, and it will be ready to use in your games.

Draw the Ruby

The first thing you'll draw in your empty window is the ruby. You have the ruby image file in your game folder, but your WhackARuby class doesn't know about it yet. Gosu supplies you with a class for handling images, named Gosu::Image. In your initialize() method, create an instance of Gosu::Image and load your ruby image into it.

Add a line of code at the end of the initialize() method that loads the image file into your game. Make sure this line is inside the initialize() method, right after the line where the caption is set, and before the end that ends the initialize() method.

Instance variable names always start with an @ symbol and are variables that are accessible from all the methods in a class. To create the variable in the initialize() method and use it in another method, you need to make it an instance variable. As your games get more complex, you'll be making a lot of instance variables.

```
WhackARuby/WhackARuby_1/whack_a_ruby.rb
def initialize
  super(800, 600)
  self.caption = 'Whack the Ruby!'
➤ @image = Gosu::Image.new('ruby.png')
end
```

The new line of code is shown *highlighted*, with an arrow pointing to it. The rest of the code you've already written; it is shown here so you can see where to put the new line.

Next, add a new method to the WhackARuby class, called draw(). The draw() method is a special method in Gosu that is run automatically when you give the final command window.show. In the draw() method of WhackARuby, you use the draw() method of @image, the instance variable you created for the ruby.

It can be confusing at first to have two methods named draw(). The draw() method of WhackARuby is going to draw all the things in your game. The draw() method of @image is going to draw just the image of the ruby. Each image in your game belongs to a separate instance of Gosu::Image, which you use to draw that image.

When you use the draw() method of Gosu::Image, you need to specify *where* you want Gosu to draw the image by providing three *arguments*. Two arguments give the location where you want the image—the first is how many pixels horizontally from the left edge of the window, and the second is how many pixels vertically from the top of the window. From now on, you'll call these numbers *x* and *y*, like the position of a point on a graph. They are a little different from the coordinates you might be used to from math class, since the y value is measured *down from the top*, rather than up from the bottom. The third number tells Gosu how to layer images on top of each other, which you need to think about when you have more than one image. The following figure shows the placement of an image in the window.

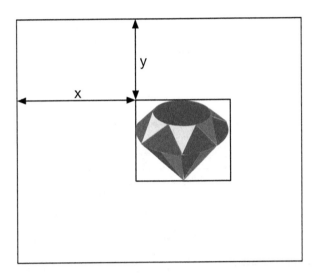

As shown in the figure, the position you give Gosu is where Gosu places the top-left corner of the image. For an image such as ruby.png that doesn't look rectangular, the position indicates the top-left corner of a rectangle that holds the image. This bounding rectangle is shown in the previous image but does not appear in your game window. The computer treats all images as rectangular, even ones that are a different shape.

You store these positions, x and y, as instance variables in your game. You set their *initial* values, @x and @y, in the initialize() method after the line that creates the @image instance variable. The lines you add here to the initialize() method are highlighted.

WhackARuby/WhackARuby_1/whack_a_ruby.rb
```ruby
def initialize
  super(800, 600)
  self.caption = 'Whack the Ruby!'
  @image = Gosu::Image.new('ruby.png')
➤ @x = 200
➤ @y = 200
end
```

One thing you need to do in many games is to find the *distance* between objects to see whether they overlap. This will be much easier if the variables @x and @y represent the position of the center of the ruby, rather than its top-left corner. You can do this by changing the values you send to the draw() method. Instead of sending @x, you send @x - @width / 2, where @width is the *for draw method, not initializing* width of your image. Likewise, you send @y - @height / 2 for the value of y. By doing this, your image will be centered on @x, @y, as shown in the following picture.

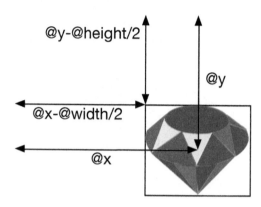

Set the initial values of @width and @height in the initialize() method. These values are the width and height of the ruby image, measured in pixels. Add these lines just after the lines that create the position variables and before the end of the initialize() method.

WhackARuby/WhackARuby_1/whack_a_ruby.rb

```
def initialize
  super(800, 600)
  self.caption = 'Whack the Ruby!'
  @image = Gosu::Image.new('ruby.png')
  @x = 200      ← just (@x, @y)
  @y = 200
➤  @width = 50
➤  @height = 43
end
```

Then add the draw() method to WhackARuby. Put def draw just after the end of the initialize() method. Make sure the end of the WhackARuby class is after the end of the draw() method.

WhackARuby/WhackARuby_1/whack_a_ruby.rb

```
def draw
    @image.draw(@x - @width / 2, @y - @height / 2, 1)
end
```

When you run the program now, you can see the ruby. It just sits there sparkling, inviting us to hit it! Before we do, we'll make it move and blink, so it's harder to hit.

Ruby Refresher: Methods Are Like Functions

If you're coming to Ruby from another language, such as Java or JavaScript, you might be used to referring to named blocks of code as functions. In Ruby, methods fill the same role, and they can have parameters and return values. We'll be writing a lot of methods, but if you've written functions in some other language, you'll find that methods are very similar.

One thing you might notice is that two different methods can have the same name. In our game, the WhackARuby class has a method called draw(), and the Gosu::Image class has a method called draw(). In the line of code @image.draw, Ruby knows to use the draw() inside Gosu::Image, since @image is of type Gosu::Image. We sometimes say @image *is a* Gosu::Image.

The draw() method of the WhackARuby class is *inherited* from the Gosu::Window class. It has a special role in Gosu games, which is discussed in the next section.

Move the Ruby

What do we mean, in a game like this one, when we say we want to move something? A video game is like a movie in that it basically fools the user into seeing motion by showing a rapid sequence of pictures in which some things are in a slightly different position. We call these pictures *frames*. If an image on our screen changes position too far between one frame and the next, it doesn't look like it is moving; it looks like it is jumping around.

Velocity

To give the ruby image the appearance of smooth motion, you can change its position by the same amount every frame. This amount is called the *velocity*. To move the ruby in the horizontal direction, change the value of @x. To move it in the vertical direction, change the value of @y. You can create two new variables, @velocity_x and @velocity_y, to keep track of the velocity. The following image shows the position of the ruby over several frames of the game. Each frame, the ruby moves @velocity_x to the right and @velocity_y down.

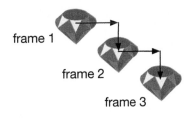

frame 1

frame 2

frame 3

This picture exaggerates the velocity to clearly show how we move the ruby. Your actual velocity is much smaller than the size of the ruby, so the ruby of each frame overlaps where the ruby was in the previous frame. You create the velocity variables in the initialize() method, after the lines that set the ruby's width and height.

WhackARuby/WhackARuby_1/whack_a_ruby.rb

```ruby
def initialize
  super(800, 600)
  self.caption = 'Whack the Ruby!'
  @image = Gosu::Image.new('ruby.png')
  @x = 200
  @y = 200
  @width = 50
  @height = 43
➤ @velocity_x = 5
➤ @velocity_y = 5
end
```

Our game has two methods so far, initialize() and draw(). A third Gosu method, update(), steps forward through the frames of our game, making our ruby move.

Update Means Animate

Window Class

The update() method is where you move your objects and handle many user actions, such as mouse clicks and key presses. When you run your Gosu project, the initialize() method runs once; then the update() and draw() methods run over and over until our game is done. This is shown in the figure. As long as the computer can keep up, these methods run sixty times per second.

In update(), you can change the values of @x and @y. You add @velocity_x to @x, and @velocity_y to @y. Add the update method after the initialize() method and before the draw() method.

WhackARuby/WhackARuby_1/whack_a_ruby.rb

```ruby
def update
  @x += @velocity_x
  @y += @velocity_y
end
```

When you run the game now, the ruby moves, but it moves right off the screen. You want the ruby to bounce off the edges of the screen, which means you have to check in your update() method to see when the image gets to an edge.

When it does, you reverse its velocity in that direction. If the image reaches the right edge, you want it to keep moving down but stop moving to the right and start moving to the left, as shown in the following figure.

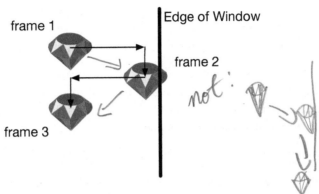

In the figure, the ruby overlaps the edge of the window in frame 2. It then reverses direction. Between frame 2 and frame 3, it moves to the left. Once again, the distance the ruby moves in each frame is exaggerated to make the figure clear. Because the ruby moves only a small number of pixels each frame, the ruby doesn't ever overlap the edge of the window very much, and the player sees the ruby bounce off the edge of the window.

To make the ruby reverse directions at the right edge, change @velocity_x from positive to negative. In the update() method, just after you move the ruby, check to see whether the ruby overlaps the window's edge. The ruby is over the edge of the window if the value of @y plus half the width of the ruby image is greater than the width of the window. When this happens, you multiply @velocity_x by -1. When the ruby overlaps the left edge, you change @velocity_x from negative to positive in the same way. You change @velocity_y when the ruby reaches the top or the bottom of the screen.

WhackARuby/WhackARuby_1/whack_a_ruby.rb
```
def update
  @x += @velocity_x
  @y += @velocity_y
  @velocity_x *= -1 if @x + @width / 2 > 800 || @x - @width / 2 < 0
  @velocity_y *= -1 if @y + @height / 2 > 600 || @y - @height / 2 < 0
end
```

When you run the game now, the ruby moves and bounces off the edges. You did it with the Gosu run loop, some instance variables, and a little math. Try making a few changes. How would you make the ruby move more slowly or more quickly?

Make the Ruby Blink

We want our ruby to be invisible most of the time and then pop onto our screen for a fraction of a second, during which time we try to whack it with the mouse. As is often the case, to add a feature you start by adding a new instance variable. You create the variable in the initialize() method, use it and change it in the update() method, and check it in the draw() method, since it affects whether you draw the ruby.

The instance variable is called @visible and is an integer. The ruby is visible and hittable when @visible is positive, and it's hidden when @visible is negative. When you make it visible, you set its value to 30. Then you decrease it by one every frame. This means that each time the ruby becomes visible, it will remain visible for 30 frames and then will become invisible again. After the ruby has been invisible for 10 frames, there is a small chance that the ruby will reappear each frame.

To do this in code, you make changes in all three methods. First, inside the initialize() method, create the @visible variable. Inside the method means that it goes after def initialize and before the end that ends the method. Generally, you add it after the other code that you've already put in the method, though often it won't really matter. When the method executes, the code is run in the order you write it.

WhackARuby/WhackARuby_1/whack_a_ruby.rb

```
def initialize
  super(800, 600)
  self.caption = 'Whack the Ruby!'
  @image = Gosu::Image.new('ruby.png')
  @x = 200
  @y = 200
  @velocity_x = 5
  @velocity_y = 5
➤ @visible = 0
end
```

In the update() method, you decrease the value of @visible. If visible is negative and has been for 10 frames, there is a small chance (1 percent) that the ruby becomes visible for 30 frames. Add the highlighted code inside the update() method.

WhackARuby/WhackARuby_1/whack_a_ruby.rb

```
def update
  @x += @velocity_x
  @y += @velocity_y
  @velocity_x *= -1 if @x + @width / 2 > 800 || @x - @width / 2 < 0
```

```
    @velocity_y *= -1 if @y + @height / 2 > 600 || @y - @height / 2 < 0
➤   @visible -= 1
➤   @visible = 30 if @visible < -10 && rand < 0.01
  end
```

In the draw() method, check to see whether @visible is positive and draw the ruby only if it is. Replace the draw() method with the following:

WhackARuby/WhackARuby_1/whack_a_ruby.rb
```
def draw
  if @visible > 0
    @image.draw(@x - @width / 2, @y - @height / 2, 1)
  end
end
```

Now the ruby blinks in and out as it moves around the screen. Later, you can adjust some of the numerical values you've used in order to balance the game and make it more fun.

Add the Hammer

To whack the ruby, we use a hammer. You draw the hammer image in the window and have it follow the player's mouse. The player tries to track the motion of the ruby by moving the hammer. Then, when the ruby becomes visible, bam! The player clicks the mouse, and you detect whether the position of the mouse click is close enough to the position of the ruby for a hit.

Drawing the hammer is similar to drawing the ruby. In the initialize() method, you make an instance variable for the hammer image and load the image file.

WhackARuby/WhackARuby_1/whack_a_ruby.rb
```
def initialize
  super(800, 600)
  self.caption = 'Whack the Ruby!'
  @image = Gosu::Image.new('ruby.png')
  @x = 200
  @y = 200
  @width = 50
  @height = 43
  @velocity_x = 5
  @velocity_y = 5
  @visible = 0
➤ @hammer_image = Gosu::Image.new('hammer.png')
  end
```

Make sure you've copied hammer.png from the book's source code into your WhackARuby folder. If the file is not there, Ruby will let you know with an error message.

Next, you draw the hammer image at the position of the mouse. You can get the position of the mouse by using two methods that Gosu gives you through the Gosu::Window class, mouse_x() and mouse_y(). These methods return the position of the mouse within the window. To draw the hammer roughly centered on the position of the mouse, draw the image just as you did the ruby image, offset by half the width of the image in the x direction and half the height in the y direction. Put the following in the draw() method.

WhackARuby/WhackARuby_1/whack_a_ruby.rb
```ruby
def draw
  if @visible > 0
    @image.draw(@x - @width / 2, @y - @height / 2, 1)
  end
➤   @hammer_image.draw(mouse_x - 40, mouse_y - 10, 1)
end
```

When you run the program now, the hammer will appear at the mouse location. If you move the mouse outside the window, the hammer won't get drawn. Move the mouse back into the window and you'll see the hammer again.

Detecting Mouse Clicks

In the update() method, you check to see whether the mouse click is close enough to the ruby. For now, make "close enough" equal to 50 pixels; you can change that later if it doesn't feel right. Use the built-in class method Gosu.distance() to see whether the click is less than 50 pixels from the center of the ruby. If it is, you've got a hit. When you hit the ruby, you want the screen to flash green, and when you miss, it should flash red. Use a new instance variable, @hit, to keep track. Normally, @hit is 0. But if you get a hit, you change it to 1, and if you miss, you change it to -1. Set @hit in the update() method, and check it in the draw() method. As with the other instance variables, you create @hit and give it an initial value in the initialize() method.

```ruby
def initialize
  super(800, 600)
  self.caption = 'Whack the Ruby!'
  @image = Gosu::Image.new('ruby.png')
  @x = 200
  @y = 200
  @width = 50
  @height = 43
  @velocity_x = 5
  @velocity_y = 5
  @visible = 0
  @hammer_image = Gosu::Image.new('hammer.png')
➤   @hit = 0
end
```

To handle the mouse click, you can use another special method of Gosu::Window. The button_down() method runs whenever you press any key or click the mouse. Gosu includes support for game pads, so you can also detect game-pad button presses. In the button_down() method, first check to see whether the button is the left mouse button. If it is, then check to see whether the position of the mouse is within 50 pixels of the position of the ruby. If this is also true, set @hit to 1. If not, set @hit to -1.

```ruby
def button_down(id)
  if (id == Gosu::MsLeft)
    if Gosu.distance(mouse_x, mouse_y, @x, @y) < 50 && @visible >= 0
      @hit = 1
    else
      @hit = -1
    end
  end
end
```

In the draw() method, we check the @hit variable. If it is -1 or 1, set a color and then fill the screen with that color using the draw_quad() method. The draw_quad() method requires twelve parameters and draws a quadrilateral—a four-sided shape. For each of the four corners of the quadrilateral, you provide the x coordinate, the y coordinate, and the color. ← *for each corner??*

The position of the top-left corner is x = 0 y = 0. The other corners are at x = 800 y = 0, x = 800 y = 600, and x = 0 y = 600.

Once you set the color c, you're ready to use draw_quad() to fill the screen with color. After you've drawn the rectangle of color, you set @hit back to 0 so it switches back to black the next time the draw() method runs.

WhackARuby/WhackARuby_1/whack_a_ruby.rb

```ruby
def draw

  if @visible > 0
    @image.draw(@x - @width / 2, @y - @height / 2, 1)
  end
  @hammer_image.draw(mouse_x - 40, mouse_y - 10, 1)
  if @hit == 0
    c = Gosu::Color::NONE
  elsif @hit == 1
    c = Gosu::Color::GREEN
  elsif @hit == -1
    c = Gosu::Color::RED
  end
  draw_quad(0, 0, c, 800, 0, c, 800, 600, c, 0, 600, c)
  @hit = 0
end
```

Run the game now and try to hit the ruby. When you get a hit, the screen will flash green, and when you miss, the screen will flash red. It's starting to look like a game.

What If It Doesn't Work?

The draw_quad() method takes a lot of parameters. If you leave just one of them off or put them in the wrong order, you get an error. See whether you can spot this one:

```
draw_quad(0, 0, c, 800, 0, c, 800, 600, c, 0, c)
```

Did you find the problem? One number is left off, near the end. When you run the game, you get an error.

```
/Users/mark/Desktop/WhackARuby/whack_a_ruby.rb:102: in `draw_quad': wrong #
of arguments(11 for 12) (ArgumentError)
  from /Users/mark/Desktop/WhackARuby/whack_a_ruby.rb:102 in `draw'
  from /Users/mark/Desktop/WhackARuby/whack_a_ruby.rb:124 in `<main>'
[Finished in 1.5s with exit code 1]
```

This one is pretty informative. It tells us that the error is on either line 102 or 124, and it tells us the problem. We have the wrong number of arguments, eleven instead of twelve, when we call draw_quad(). We try to fix it by adding another number at the end, so it looks like this:

```
draw_quad(0, 0, c, 800, 0, c, 800, 600, c, 0, c, 600)
```

Unfortunately, we have a different error now:

```
/Users/mark/Desktop/WhackARuby/whack_a_ruby.rb:102: in `draw_quad':
Expected argument 11 of type double, but got
Gosu::Color #<Gosu::Color:0x007fcf4202da78... (TypeError)
in SWIG method 'drawQuad'
  from /Users/mark/Desktop/WhackARuby/whack_a_ruby.rb:102: in `draw'
  from /Users/mark/Desktop/WhackARuby/whack_a_ruby.rb:124: in `<main>'
[Finished in 1.3s with exit code 1]
```

The error is still on the same line, but now argument 11 is the wrong type, Gosu::Color instead of double. You need to put the arguments in the correct order—two numbers and a color, in that order—for each of the four corners of the rectangle.

Keep Score

Keeping track of the player's score is one way to make Whack-A-Ruby a game. Players can try to beat their friends' scores or their own previous best score. They can brag about their high score and post it on social media.

In Whack-A-Ruby, we start with zero points. Every time we whack the ruby, let's add five points, and every time we miss, we'll take away one point.

You draw the score on the screen using another Gosu class, Gosu::Font. To create an instance of Gosu::Font, you tell Gosu what size characters you want in the window. The size of the font is the height of the tallest character in pixels. In the initialize() method, you create your @font instance variable, along with another variable to keep track of the score.

```
WhackARuby/WhackARuby_1/whack_a_ruby.rb
def initialize
  super(800, 600)
  self.caption = 'Whack the Ruby!'
  @image = Gosu::Image.new('ruby.png')
  @x = 200
  @y = 200
  @width = 50
  @height = 43
  @velocity_x = 5
  @velocity_y = 5
  @visible = 0
  @hammer_image = Gosu::Image.new('hammer.png')
  @hit = 0
➤ @font = Gosu::Font.new(30)
➤ @score = 0
end
```

You already check to see whether you hit the ruby in button_down(id). You can add and subtract from the @score variable here:

```
WhackARuby/WhackARuby_1/whack_a_ruby.rb
def button_down(id)
  if (id == Gosu::MsLeft)
    if Gosu.distance(mouse_x, mouse_y, @x, @y) < 50 && @visible >= 0
      @hit = 1
➤     @score += 5
    else
      @hit = -1
➤     @score -= 1
    end
  end
end
```

Then you draw the score, using the draw() method of Gosu::Font. Pass in the string you want to draw, which in this case is the score. Because the score is an integer, convert it to a string. You also supply the position of the score on the screen. This goes in the draw() method:

```
WhackARuby/WhackARuby_1/whack_a_ruby.rb
def draw
  if @visible > 0
    @image.draw(@x - @width / 2, @y - @height / 2, 1)
  end
  @hammer_image.draw(mouse_x - 40, mouse_y - 10, 1)
  if @hit == 0
```

```
    c = Gosu::Color::NONE
  elsif @hit == 1
    c = Gosu::Color::GREEN
  elsif @hit == -1
    c = Gosu::Color::RED
  end
  draw_quad(0, 0, c, 800, 0, c, 800, 600, c, 0, 600, c)
  @hit = 0
➤ @font.draw(@score.to_s, 700, 20, 2)
end
```

position

We're getting close to being done. But if you play now, you can play forever
and eventually get any score you want.

Set a Time Limit

120? 150?

To make the game competitive, let's give the player 100 seconds to play. That
way, a higher score indicates more skill, not just more patience.

Gosu has a class method Gosu.milliseconds() that returns the number of millisec-
onds since the game started. You use this method to calculate how many
seconds the player has been playing, and subtract that from 100. In the
update() method, you figure out how many seconds remain and convert it to a
string:

WhackARuby/WhackARuby_1/whack_a_ruby.rb
```
def update
  @x += @velocity_x
  @y += @velocity_y
  @velocity_x *= -1 if @x + @width / 2 > 800 || @x - @width / 2 < 0
  @velocity_y *= -1 if @y + @height / 2 > 600 || @y - @height / 2 < 0
  @visible -= 1
  @visible = 30 if @visible < -10 && rand < 0.01
➤ @time_left = (100 - (Gosu.milliseconds / 1000))
end
```

You can display this on the screen using the @font instance. As long as you
want the same font and size, you don't need a new instance of Gosu::Font; you
can reuse the one you already have. In the draw() method, draw the @time_left
string.

WhackARuby/WhackARuby_1/whack_a_ruby.rb
```
def draw
  if @visible > 0
    @image.draw(@x - @width / 2, @y - @height / 2, 1)
  end
  @hammer_image.draw(mouse_x - 40, mouse_y - 10, 1)
  if @hit == 0
    c = Gosu::Color::NONE
```

```
      elsif @hit == 1
        c = Gosu::Color::GREEN
      elsif @hit == -1
        c = Gosu::Color::RED
      end
      draw_quad(0, 0, c, 800, 0, c, 800, 600, c, 0, 600, c)
      @hit = 0
➤     @font.draw(@time_left.to_s, 20, 20, 2)
    end
```

When you run the program now, the time counts down from 100. If we play long enough now, the time remaining becomes negative. We need to stop the countdown and end the game.

Game Over!

For our first game, we want to end it very simply. When the clock reaches zero, let's stop all movement, show the ruby, and write "Game Over" in the center of the screen. You use a Boolean instance variable, @playing, to keep track of when the game is over. Create this variable and set its value to true in the initialize() method:

WhackARuby/WhackARuby_2/whack_a_ruby.rb
```
def initialize
  super(800,600)
  self.caption = 'Whack the Ruby!'
  @image = Gosu::Image.new('ruby.png')
  @x = 200
  @y = 200
  @width = 50
  @height = 43
  @velocity_x = 5
  @velocity_y = 5
  @visible = 0
  @hammer_image = Gosu::Image.new('hammer.png')
  @hit = 0
  @score = 0
  @font = Gosu::Font.new(30)
➤ @playing = true
end
```

In the update() method, check the value of @playing. If its value is true, you do all the things you were doing before. If the value of @playing is false, you don't do anything at all. Also check to see how much time has elapsed using Gosu.milliseconds(). If 100 seconds have elapsed, set @playing to false.

WhackARuby/WhackARuby_2/whack_a_ruby.rb

```
def update
➤   if @playing
      @x += @velocity_x
      @y += @velocity_y
      @visible -= 1
      @velocity_x *= -1 if @x + @width / 2 > 800 || @x - @width / 2 < 0
      @velocity_y *= -1 if @y + @height / 2 > 600 || @y - @height / 2 < 0
      @visible = 30 if @visible < -10 && rand < 0.01
      @time_left = (100 - ((Gosu.milliseconds - @start_time) / 1000))
➤     @playing = false if @time_left < 0
➤   end
end
```

In the button_down() method, you use the same pattern and check to see whether you've clicked the mouse only when @playing is true:

WhackARuby/WhackARuby_2/whack_a_ruby.rb

```
def button_down(id)
➤   if @playing
      if id == Gosu::MsLeft
        if Gosu.distance(mouse_x, mouse_y, @x, @y) < 50 && @visible >= 0
          @hit = 1
          @score += 5
        else
          @hit = -1
          @score -= 1
        end
      end
➤   end
end
```

In the draw() method, add the code that draws the "Game Over" message:

WhackARuby/WhackARuby_2/whack_a_ruby.rb

```
def draw
  if @visible > 0
    @image.draw(@x - @width / 2, @y - @height / 2, 1)
  end
  @hammer_image.draw(mouse_x - 40, mouse_y - 10, 1)
  if @hit == 0
    c = Gosu::Color::NONE
  elsif @hit == 1
    c = Gosu::Color::GREEN
  elsif @hit == -1
    c = Gosu::Color::RED
  end
  draw_quad(0, 0, c, 800, 0, c, 800, 600, c, 0, 600, c)
  @hit = 0
  @font.draw(@time_left.to_s, 20, 20, 2)
  @font.draw(@score.to_s, 700, 20, 2)
```

```
➤    unless @playing
➤      @font.draw('Game Over', 300, 300, 3)
➤      @visible = 20
➤    end
    end
```

We're almost finished. When the game ends now, we have to quit the game to play again. Instead, let's allow the player to press a key to play again.

Play Again?

Let's add a "Press the Space Bar to Play Again" message and set up the game to play again. You need to set the score back to 0 and give the player a new 100 seconds to play. You add the new message to the screen in the draw() method when the game is over:

```
WhackARuby/WhackARuby_2/whack_a_ruby.rb
def draw
  if @visible > 0
    @image.draw(@x - @width / 2, @y - @height / 2, 1)
  end
  @hammer_image.draw(mouse_x - 40, mouse_y - 10, 1)
  if @hit == 0
    c = Gosu::Color::NONE
  elsif @hit == 1
    c = Gosu::Color::GREEN
  elsif @hit == -1
    c = Gosu::Color::RED
  end
  draw_quad(0, 0, c, 800, 0, c, 800, 600, c, 0, 600, c)
  @hit = 0
  @font.draw(@time_left.to_s, 20, 20, 2)
  @font.draw(@score.to_s, 700, 20, 2)
  unless @playing
    @font.draw('Game Over', 300, 300, 3)
➤    @font.draw('Press the Space Bar to Play Again', 175, 350, 3)
    @visible = 20
  end
```

When you calculate the time, you've been using the Gosu.milliseconds() method, assuming the start time of the game is 0. When you restart the game, Gosu.milliseconds() no longer tells you how long you've been playing. To adjust for this, add a new instance variable called @start_time that keeps track of when the current game started. In the initialize() method, create that variable and set it to 0:

WhackARuby/WhackARuby_2/whack_a_ruby.rb
```ruby
def initialize
  super(800,600)
  self.caption = 'Whack the Ruby!'
  @image = Gosu::Image.new('ruby.png')
  @x = 200
  @y = 200
  @width = 50
  @height = 43
  @velocity_x = 5
  @velocity_y = 5
  @visible = 0
  @hammer_image = Gosu::Image.new('hammer.png')
  @hit = 0
  @score = 0
  @font = Gosu::Font.new(30)
  @playing = true
➤  @start_time = 0

end
```

Then change both references to Gosu.milliseconds() in the update() method to subtract the start time. That difference, Gosu.milliseconds - @start_time, is the elapsed time of the current game:

WhackARuby/WhackARuby_3/whack_a_ruby.rb
```ruby
def update
  if @playing
    @x += @velocity_x
    @y += @velocity_y
    @visible -= 1
➤    @time_left = (100 - ((Gosu.milliseconds - @start_time) / 1000))
➤    @playing = false if @time_left < 0
    @velocity_x *= -1 if @x + @width/2 > 800 || @x - @width / 2 < 0
    @velocity_y *= -1 if @y + @height/2 > 600 || @y - @height / 2 < 0
    @visible = 30 if @visible < -10 and rand < 0.01
  end
end
```

Run the program now and make sure that it behaves the same as it did before.

Next, change the button_down() method so that it checks for the spacebar, but only when @playing is false. When the user presses the spacebar, you reset the game and set @start_time to the current value of Gosu.milliseconds():

WhackARuby/WhackARuby_3/whack_a_ruby.rb
```ruby
def button_down(id)
  if @playing
    if (id == Gosu::MsLeft)
      if Gosu.distance(mouse_x, mouse_y, @x, @y) < 50 && @visible >= 0
        @hit = 1
```

```
        @score += 5
      else
        @hit = -1
        @score -= 1
      end
    end
  else
    if (id == Gosu::KbSpace)
      @playing = true
      @visible = -10
      @start_time = Gosu.milliseconds
      @score = 0
    end
  end
end
```

And your first game is complete. Now you should play for a while and show your friends the game you've made. While you're playing, think about what you find annoying and what would make the game more challenging. One of the best things about the games you write yourself is that you can change everything about them. Your game is complete, but it may not be *done*.

Make It Your Own

While we made the Whack-A-Ruby game, we made many choices: how fast the ruby moves, how long it stays visible, and with what chance it reappears. Is 100 seconds too long or too short? The game might be too hard or too easy. Change the game until you're happy with it. Make it your game! Here are some changes you could make, in no particular order:

Make the ruby appear for a shorter or longer time.
Figure out which number determines how many frames the ruby is visible and change the number.

Make the ruby appear more or less often.
Figure out which number determines how often the ruby becomes visible and change it.

Change the images to something else.
Add the images to the game folder. Look in the code for filenames and pay attention to image sizes.

Add another ruby bouncing around that you can click.
You need duplicates for a whole bunch of instance variables. Maybe name them @x_2, @velocity_y_2, and so on. This one is challenging!

Add another thing that bounces around that you can't click. Maybe an emerald?
You need another image and some new instance variables.

Make "Game Over" appear in a larger font.
Make another instance variable for a different-sized font.

What's Next

In Whack-A-Ruby, your goal was to learn how Gosu works, and you made a working game. You put all your code in the WhackARuby class, and it started to get a little long, even for this simple game. For your next game, you'll separate the code out into more classes, one for each type of object in the game. This will prove to be a powerful tool, especially when you want to have many objects on the screen at once.

CHAPTER 4

Creating a Sprite-Based Game

Many video games—from old classics such as *Asteroids* and *Pac-Man*, to modern mobile games such as *Flappy Bird* and *Temple Run*—are made using *sprites*. Sprite is a term that dates back to 1970s video game systems like the Atari. It refers to a small image that moves around inside a scene. In a single game there can be many sprites; often one sprite is controlled by the player, and others are controlled by the program.

We're going to make our own sprite-based game called Sector Five, in which the player moves a spaceship around the screen by pressing keys. Waves of enemy ships descend from above, and the player needs to shoot them before they get to the bottom of the screen and destroy the player's base. When we're finished, it will look like this.

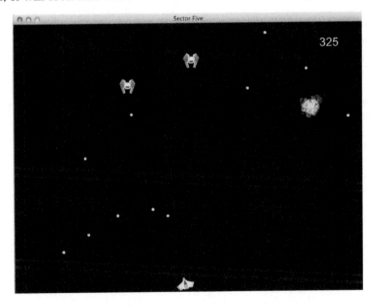

Sector Five has four different kinds of sprites. One is a spaceship, controlled by the player. Enemy ships are sprites that descend from the top of the screen. Bullet sprites appear when the player presses the spacebar and move in a straight line from the player ship. And animated explosion sprites appear when the bullets hit enemy ships. Each kind of sprite acts differently, and each has a Ruby *class* to describe its behavior. Once we've written the class that describes what a sprite can do, we'll create *instances* of that class, one for each object in our game.

Sector Five is a more complicated and ambitious game than Whack-A-Ruby, and we'll be working on this game for three chapters. In this chapter you'll learn to:

- Create classes to represent different kinds of sprites.

- Use those classes to create sprites in your window.

- Move a sprite by pressing the keys.

- Use constants to adjust the play of your game and make it more challenging.

In the next chapter, you'll learn how to add piles of enemy ships, all based on one class, and how to tell when sprites collide with each other. In the final chapter on Sector Five, you'll learn how to add sound effects to your game. When you're finished, you'll have all the tools you need to create your own sprite-based games.

Start by copying the folder called SectorFive_starter from the source folder you downloaded earlier into your Games folder. It has the images and sounds for all three chapters' worth of Sector Five. It also has a file, sector_five.rb, that creates a window, just like the one we started with in Whack-A-Ruby.

SectorFive/SectorFive_starter/sector_five.rb

```ruby
require 'gosu'

class SectorFive < Gosu::Window
  def initialize
    super(800, 600)
    self.caption = 'Sector Five'
  end
end

window = SectorFive.new
window.show
```

This window is where you'll create, move, and draw your sprites. Run this program to make sure all is well. An empty window will open on your screen. The first sprite you'll add is a spaceship for the player to fly around the screen.

The Player Class

Each sprite class in Sector Five manages one kind of sprite. A sprite class is a collection of *instance variables* that store information about the sprite, and *methods*, which are commands you give the sprite. When you're creating a new sprite class, make a list of the information the sprite needs to store and the commands you want it to follow. The player ship sprite stores an image and a position. Because it can rotate, it also stores the angle through which its image has turned. The commands the ship follows include "turn right," "turn left," and "draw." A class diagram shows the instance variables and methods for a class in a box. Here is one for the Player class:

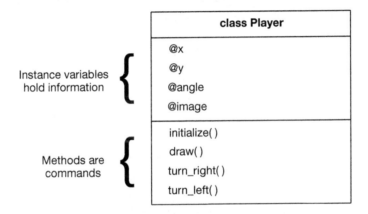

The initialize() method is not really a command to the ship, but it's included in the diagram because without it, there won't even be a ship.

You'll create and test the Player class one piece at a time to learn how these variables and methods work. Later, when you've had more experience, you might write most of a sprite class before you test its methods.

Create a new file, player.rb, in the same folder as your game file, sector_five.rb.

First add just enough to player.rb so that you can create and draw the ship image. To get there, create the initialize() and draw() methods of the Player class. Then, in your SectorFive class, you'll use those methods. In the initialize() method, you just say "Make a new ship, based on class Player, and store it in the @player variable." Then, when it's time to draw the ship, you just tell @player to execute its draw() method.

In the initialize() method of the Player class, you create and set some instance variables. Set the position of the ship, just as you did for the ruby in Whack-A-Ruby. Create an image variable using the file ship.png in the images folder. The initialize() method takes one argument, a reference to the window, which you'll use later to let the ship interact with the window edges.

SectorFive/SectorFive_1/player.rb
```
class Player
  def initialize(window)
    @x = 200
    @y = 200
    @angle = 0
    @image = Gosu::Image.new('images/ship.png')
  end
end
```

In the draw() method of the Player class, use a new method of Gosu::Image, draw_rot(). This method draws the image rotated by any angle, measured in degrees. Put the draw() method after the initialize() method:

SectorFive/SectorFive_1/player.rb
```
def draw
  @image.draw_rot(@x, @y, 1, @angle)
end
```

Another useful thing about the draw_rot() method is that it centers the image on the x and y values you send as the first two parameters.

Back in SectorFive, you can now use these methods to add and draw the player. First, include your new code in the sector_five.rb file, using require_relative. This line goes just after require gosu and before your SectorFive class. When some of the code is highlighted with arrows, only the highlighted code is new—the rest is there to help you figure out where to put the new code.

SectorFive/SectorFive_1/sector_five.rb
```
  require 'gosu'
➤ require_relative 'player'
```

In the initialize() method of SectorFive, create the ship:

SectorFive/SectorFive_1/sector_five.rb
```
  def initialize
    super(800, 600)
    self.caption = "Sector Five"
➤   @player = Player.new(self)
  end
```

Notice that you send self as a parameter to the initialize() method. The initialize() method of Player takes the window as an argument. In the SectorFive class, the window is self, so that's what you pass to Player.new(). You'll do the same thing each time you create a new sprite.

The SectorFive class now gets a draw() method, where you'll eventually draw all the sprites in the game. For now, just draw the player ship:

SectorFive/SectorFive_1/sector_five.rb
```
def draw
  @player.draw
end
```

Before you run the game, if you're running right from your editor, make sure the sector_five.rb file is open in the front window or tab. If you run and nothing happens, you've likely got the player.rb file at the front. When you run the game, your ship will appear, as shown in the following picture:

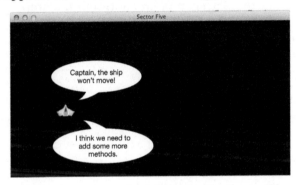

We've gotten our ship to appear, but it just sits there. We want to let the player move it around, not with the mouse, but using the keyboard.

What If It Doesn't Work?

Now that your program consists of more than one file, errors you make can be in either file. Maybe while following the tutorial you accidentally put the code for Player.draw() in sector_five.rb. Hopefully you'd see that you had two methods named draw() in SectorFive, but what if you missed this? When you run the game this way, you get this error:

```
/Users/mark/Desktop/SectorFive_1/sector_five.rb:13: in `draw':
undefined method `draw_rot' for nil:Nil (NoMethodError) from
/Users/mark/Desktop/SectorFive_1/sector_five.rb:18: in `main'
```

The error is on the line that says @image.draw_rot(@x, @y, 1, @angle). The real clue is that Ruby sees that the method draw_rot() has been called on something that is nil. @image is nil, since it is not instantiated in SectorFive. The problem is that @image doesn't belong to SectorFive, but rather to Player. Don't give up reading the error messages! You'll get to understand them better and better if you keep at it.

Move the Ship

The player moves the ship by pressing three keys. Gosu treats keys exactly the same as mouse buttons and calls all of them buttons. You use the left arrow, the right arrow, and the up arrow to move the ship. The ship moves forward by firing its engines; the ship doesn't have any way to fire the engines backward. If you stop firing the engines, the ship coasts gradually to a stop.

Of course, this isn't actually realistic, but our primary goal is to make the game fun. Sometimes realistic is fun, and sometimes realistic is just frustrating. Our job as game designers is to strike the right balance. In this game, we want moving the spaceship around to be fun. We use some ideas from physics to make the ship feel like a real object that we are moving by pressing three keys. We want the player to be in control of the ship, but not in total control. The player has to develop a little skill to move the ship the way he or she wants. And that is fun!

Turn the Ship

To rotate the ship, create two methods in the Player class, turn_right() and turn_left(). These methods change the @angle variable, and so they change the way the ship is drawn.

SectorFive/SectorFive_1/player.rb
```
def turn_right
  @angle += 3
end
def turn_left
  @angle -= 3
end
```

Next, change the update() method of the SectorFive class to call turn_right() and turn_left() when you press the arrow keys. Gosu gives you access to the keys, just as it gives you access to the mouse. You might be able to figure out many of the key constants, like Gosu::KbLeft for the left arrow key or Gosu::KbA for the A key. There is a list of all the key constants in the documentation of the Gosu class, which you can find at http://www.libgosu.org/rdoc/Gosu.html.

You use a method called button_down?() to see whether each key is pressed; this method is part of the Gosu::Window class.

SectorFive/SectorFive_1/sector_five.rb
```
def update
  @player.turn_left if button_down?(Gosu::KbLeft)
  @player.turn_right if button_down?(Gosu::KbRight)
end
```

(What do you think will happen if both keys are pressed?)

Look at what we just did to add a behavior to the player ship. In the Player class, you wrote two methods, turn_right() and turn_left(). Then in the update() method of SectorFive, you called those methods when the arrow keys were pressed.

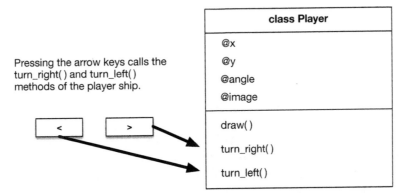

Pressing the arrow keys calls the turn_right( ) and turn_left( ) methods of the player ship.

You can run the game now and turn the ship with the arrow keys. After you spin the ship around a few times in each direction, you'll realize that it's time to get the ship moving forward.

button_down() vs. button_down?()

In Whack-A-Ruby, you used the button_down(id) method to detect mouse clicks and key presses. This method runs once for each time the button is clicked. To rotate the player ship, you use the button_down?() method, which is a different method. The question mark is part of the method name. When should you use each one?

button_down?()

Use this method when holding the button down should do something over and over. Put it in the update() method, inside a *conditional* statement. You can use this method to turn the ship; if you hold the arrow key down, the ship keeps turning.

button_down(id)

When you want the press to do something, and then not do it again until you release the button and press it again, use button_down(id). You used this method to whack the ruby, and you'll use it to fire bullets. Each key press will fire one bullet, and holding down the key won't do anything beyond the initial press. This method is separate from the update() and draw() methods and is not used inside them.

Make the Ship Accelerate

When you press the forward arrow, you want the ship to *accelerate*. Accelerate means to change the velocity. If your ship is sitting still and you press the forward arrow, it moves in the direction it is pointing, speeding up as it goes. If you turn the ship while it's moving and press the up arrow, the ship moves in a curved path, as shown in the following diagram.

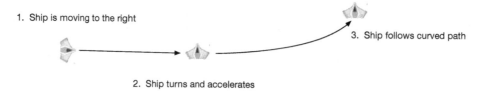

1. Ship is moving to the right

3. Ship follows curved path

2. Ship turns and accelerates

To make the ship move like this, you need to add a few new variables and a few new methods to the Player class. The variables will keep track of the ship's velocity. One method of the SectorFive class, accelerate(), will be called when you hold down the up arrow key. Another one, move(), will get called every frame, so the ship keeps moving even when you're not pressing a key.

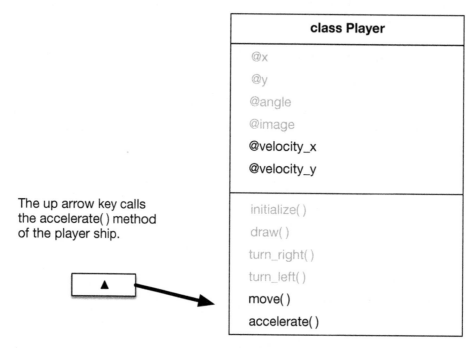

The up arrow key calls the accelerate() method of the player ship.

class Player
@x
@y
@angle
@image
@velocity_x
@velocity_y
initialize( )
draw( )
turn_right( )
turn_left( )
move( )
accelerate( )

Add the two new variables and set them to 0 in the initialize() method of the Player class.

SectorFive/SectorFive_1/player.rb
```ruby
def initialize(window)
  @x = 200
  @y = 200
  @angle = 0
  @image = Gosu::Image.new('images/ship.png')
➤ @velocity_x = 0
➤ @velocity_y = 0
end
```

In the accelerate() method, change the velocity of the ship in the direction that the ship is currently pointing. Gosu has some helper methods, offset_x() and offset_y.(), that do some of the math for you.

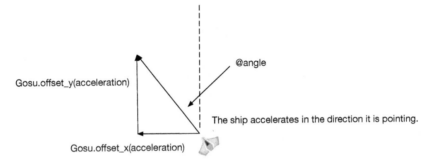

Gosu.offset_y(acceleration)

@angle

Gosu.offset_x(acceleration)

The ship accelerates in the direction it is pointing.

The offset_x() method takes the angle and an amount as arguments and returns the amount in the x direction, either positive or negative. You could do this yourself using a little trigonometry, but since games make use of these calculations so often, Gosu provides them for convenience. Use these methods to change the velocity in the accelerate() method of the Player class.

SectorFive/SectorFive_1/player.rb
```ruby
def accelerate
  @velocity_x += Gosu.offset_x(@angle, 2)
  @velocity_y += Gosu.offset_y(@angle, 2)
end
```

You change the position of the ship in the move() method of the Player class. This method is called every update, so that the ship moves even when no key is being pressed.

SectorFive/SectorFive_1/player.rb
```ruby
def move
  @x += @velocity_x
  @y += @velocity_y
  @velocity_x *= 0.9
  @velocity_y *= 0.9
end
```

In the move() method of the Player class, you also slow down the ship by multiplying the velocities by 0.9 each update. This acts like a sort of friction and makes controlling the motion of the ship a little easier.

Now that your move() and accelerate() methods are ready, you call them in the update() method of the SectorFive class. The ship moves every frame and accelerates whenever you press the up arrow.

SectorFive/SectorFive_1/sector_five.rb
```
def update
  @player.turn_left if button_down?(Gosu::KbLeft)
  @player.turn_right if button_down?(Gosu::KbRight)
➤ @player.accelerate if button_down?(Gosu::KbUp)
➤ @player.move

end
```

Because you want the ship to accelerate continuously when the arrow key is held down, you use the button_down?() method. Run the game now and move the ship around. See whether you can fly in circles. Be careful! For now, you can fly your ship right out of the window. If you do, it can be tough to get it back in.

You've added the ship to the window, and you can move it around with the arrow keys. In the SectorFive class, you detect button presses, and those button presses call methods of the @player object to tell it what to do. The diagram on page 49 shows how the Gosu methods in SectorFive work together with the methods in the sprite class to let us create, move, and draw the player ship:

Before we add more sprites to the game, we'll spend a little more time with the ship, and you'll learn how you can adjust the way it moves to suit your players.

Use Constants to Adjust Your Game

You've put several numbers into the code that determine how the motion of the ship responds to key presses. In the turn_right() and turn_left() methods, you adjust the angle by 3. In the accelerate() method, you change @velocity_x and @velocity_y, and in move() you slow the ship down. We'll use constants to gather these numbers into one place. These constants are named with all capital letters, so you can keep them separate from variables and classes. The three constants are named ROTATION_SPEED, ACCELERATION, and FRICTION.

To create the ROTATION_SPEED constant, add a line to the Player class, just after class Player and before the initialize() method:

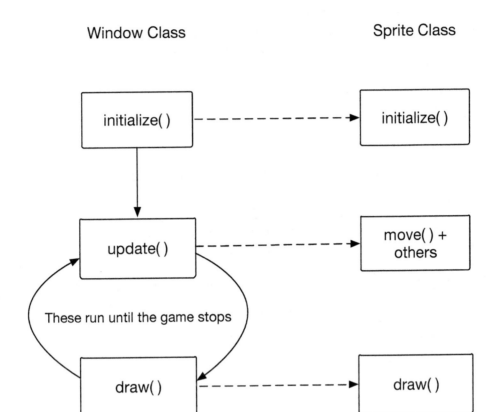

Window Class   **Sprite Class**

Figure 1—The Gosu run loop with a sprite

SectorFive/SectorFive_2/player.rb
```ruby
class Player
  ROTATION_SPEED = 3
```

Then, in the turn_right() and turn_left() methods, replace the number 3 with the constant you've created:

SectorFive/SectorFive_2/player.rb
```ruby
def turn_right
  @angle += ROTATION_SPEED
end

def turn_left
  @angle -= ROTATION_SPEED
end
```

If you run the game now, nothing has changed. But now you can change the value of ROTATION_SPEED in one place to adjust your game. Now create two more constants in the Player class, ACCELERATION and FRICTION. Put these right after the ROTATION_SPEED declaration:

SectorFive/SectorFive_2/player.rb
```
class Player
  ROTATION_SPEED = 3
➤  ACCELERATION = 2
➤  FRICTION = 0.9
```

Replace the number 2 in the accelerate() method with ACCELERATION:

SectorFive/SectorFive_2/player.rb
```
def accelerate
➤  @velocity_x += Gosu.offset_x(@angle, ACCELERATION)
➤  @velocity_y += Gosu.offset_y(@angle, ACCELERATION)
end
```

Then FRICTION replaces the number 0.9 in the move() method of the Player class:

SectorFive/SectorFive_2/player.rb
```
def move
  @x += @velocity_x
  @y += @velocity_y
➤  @velocity_x *= FRICTION
➤  @velocity_y *= FRICTION
end
```

After any or each of these replacements, you can run the game and everything should be the same.

Also create constants in the SectorFive class for the width and height of the window:

SectorFive/SectorFive_2/sector_five.rb
```
class SectorFive < Gosu::Window
➤  WIDTH = 800
➤  HEIGHT = 600
  def initialize
➤    super(WIDTH,HEIGHT)
    self.caption = 'Sector Five'
    @player = Player.new(self)
  end
```

By using constants, you get code that is a little easier to understand and a little easier to adjust. Now, if you want to adjust the rotation speed, you only have to change it in one place, not two. Naming things is often better than putting numbers right in your code.

Hitting the Edges

While flying the ship around, you probably flew the ship right out of the window at one time or another. This can be pretty frustrating, since when the ship is out of the window you can't see which way it's pointed, and it's very tough to maneuver it back into view. Think about how different games solve this problem. Some games *scroll*, so that the window actually follows the player. We'll explore this solution later in the book, in Chapter 9, *Making a Side-Scrolling Game*, on page 157. Some games *wrap*, so that if the player sprite moves off the left edge, it reappears at the right edge of the window. In Sector Five, we add bounds to our window, so that if the player ship gets to the right, left, or bottom edge of the window, the ship is stopped by the sector force fields. If the player ship ever goes off the top of the window, it is destroyed by the enemy mother ship.

For the player ship to stop at the edges, it needs to know where the edges are. You'll encounter this problem again and again, where one object—in this case, @player—needs to know some information about another object—in this case, the window. To solve this, you have @player, when it is created, save the *reference* to the window object in an instance variable called @window.

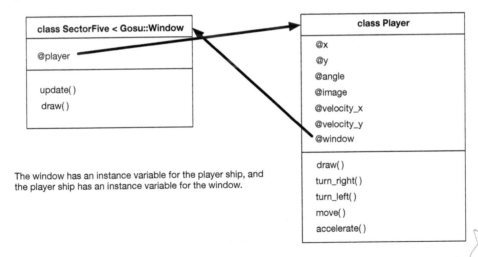

The window has an instance variable for the player ship, and the player ship has an instance variable for the window.

The ship reaches the edge when its center gets within a distance of the edge equal to the radius of the ship. So you also create an instance variable @radius in the Player class. Add these two variables in the initialize() method of the Player class:

SectorFive/SectorFive_2/player.rb
```
def initialize(window)
  @x = 200
  @y = 200
  @angle = 0
  @image = Gosu::Image.new('images/ship.png')
  @velocity_x = 0
  @velocity_y = 0
➤ @radius = 20
➤ @window = window
end
```

The Gosu::Window class has methods that let you use your @window reference to
get the width and height of the window. These methods are called width() and
height(). You handle the ship reaching the force fields by adding to the move()
method of the Player class. When the ship reaches or overshoots the edge, you
move it back to the edge and set its velocity in that direction to 0. The player
ship can still go off the top of the window. In Chapter 6, *Adding Scenes and
Sounds*, on page 79, you'll destroy the player ship and end the game when
that happens.

SectorFive/SectorFive_2/player.rb
```
def move
  @x += @velocity_x
  @y += @velocity_y
  @velocity_x *= FRICTION
  @velocity_y *= FRICTION
➤ if @x > @window.width - @radius
➤   @velocity_x = 0
➤   @x = @window.width - @radius
➤ end
➤ if @x < @radius
➤   @velocity_x = 0
➤   @x = @radius
➤ end
➤ if @y > @window.height - @radius
➤   @velocity_y = 0
➤   @y = @window.height - @radius
➤ end
end
```

Run the game now, and the player ship will stop at the left, right, and bottom
borders of the window. Next you'll add enemy ships, falling from above.

Make an Enemy

The second kind of sprite you add to the game is the enemy ship. Enemy
ships appear at the top of the screen, at a random horizontal position, and

fall straight down. You will need enough of them so that it's a challenge to shoot them all before they reach the bottom, but to write and test your enemy ship class, you'll first make just one.

The Enemy class is simpler than the Player class. Enemy ships only move down and are controlled by the computer. They don't respond directly to player actions. The Enemy class has initialize(), move(), and draw() methods as well as instance variables for its position and image. Here is the diagram for the Enemy class:

class Enemy
@x @y @image
initialize( ) draw( ) move( )

Make sure the enemy.png image is in your images folder. Then make a new file, enemy.rb, for the Enemy class in your SectorFive folder.

In the initialize() method of the Enemy class, set @y to 0, which is the top of the window. Set @x to a random number. Because @x is going to be the center of your enemy ship, and you want the whole enemy to fit in the window, the horizontal position should be a random number with a minimum value equal to the radius of the enemy and a maximum value equal to the width of the window minus the radius.

SectorFive/SectorFive_2/enemy.rb
```
class Enemy
  def initialize(window)
    @radius = 20              (max - min) + min
    @x = rand(window.width - 2 * @radius) + @radius
    @y = 0
    @image = Gosu::Image.new('images/enemy.png')
  end
end
```

You can make a random number between any two values by passing the difference between the minimum and maximum values to the rand() method and then adding the minimum value.

In the move() method, you can increase @y by the speed of the ship, which you make a constant called SPEED. Add the SPEED declaration just after class Enemy:

SectorFive/SectorFive_2/enemy.rb
```
class Enemy
➤   SPEED = 4
    def initialize(window)
      @radius = 20
      @x = rand(window.width - 2 * @radius) + @radius
      @y = 0
      @image = Gosu::Image.new('images/enemy.png')
    end
```

Then use the SPEED constant in the move() method. The enemy ship will move only in the y direction:

SectorFive/SectorFive_2/enemy.rb
```
def move
  @y += SPEED
end
```

In the draw() method of Enemy, offset the image by @radius to center the image on @x and @y:

SectorFive/SectorFive_2/enemy.rb
```
def draw
  @image.draw(@x - @radius, @y - @radius, 1)
end
```

Once the Enemy class is set up, you can create, move, and draw a single enemy with just a few lines of code in the SectorFive class. You need to include the code for the Enemy class in sector_five.rb just after you add the Player class:

SectorFive/SectorFive_2/sector_five.rb
```
require 'gosu'
require_relative 'player'
➤ require_relative 'enemy'
```

Add one new line to the initialize() method that creates a single enemy and stores it in @enemy:

SectorFive/SectorFive_2/sector_five.rb
```
def initialize
  super(WIDTH,HEIGHT)
  self.caption = 'Sector Five'
  @player = Player.new(self)
➤   @enemy = Enemy.new(self)
end
```

Move the enemy in the update() method, with another line of code:

SectorFive/SectorFive_2/sector_five.rb

```ruby
def update
  @player.turn_left if button_down?(Gosu::KbLeft)
  @player.turn_right if button_down?(Gosu::KbRight)
  @player.accelerate if button_down?(Gosu::KbUp)
  @player.move
➤ @enemy.move
end
```

Finally, draw the enemy ship in the draw() method of the SectorFive class:

SectorFive/SectorFive_2/sector_five.rb

```ruby
def draw
  @player.draw
➤ @enemy.draw
end
```

When you run the game now, a single enemy will fall from the top of the screen and off the bottom.

Make It Your Own

The game isn't finished, but this is a good time to stop and do a few experiments. *Save a copy of your entire game folder before you make any big changes.* Then try one or more of the following exercises or make something up yourself.

Change the game constants.

The constants in Player—especially ACCELERATION and FRICTION—control how the player ship moves. Even small changes in these can make a big difference in how maneuvering the ship feels. Try changing FRICTION to 1. Try changing it to 0. What happens? Can you explain why, by looking at the code? Try adjusting those constants to make controlling the ship challenging and fun.

Change the enemy ship movement.

Right now the enemy ship moves straight down. Try having it move at an angle. What should it do if it reaches an edge? All the changes should be in the Enemy class.

Make the player ship bounce.

The player ship hits the edges and the bottom now and stops. But you could make the player ship bounce off the edges instead, by changing a few lines of code in the move() method of the Player class. When the ruby in Whack-A-Ruby hit the sides of the window, it bounced off. Go back and look at that code if you've forgotten how you did that.

Make several enemies.

In the next chapter we'll be making lots of enemies, but you could increase the number to two or three right now. Make more instances of the Enemy class to create more enemies.

What's Next

In this chapter, you learned to use sprite classes to make player and enemy ships appear on the screen. You used the keyboard to move the player ship and made one enemy ship fall from above. But one enemy is not enough. In the next chapter, you'll learn how to turn one enemy into dozens, or even hundreds. You'll also make bullets and detect collisions between bullets and enemy ships. And then you'll make the enemies explode in balls of fire.

CHAPTER 5

Managing Lots of Sprites

Our Sector Five game now has only one enemy ship. In this chapter we add more, so a constant stream of enemies falls from above. Then we let our player ship shoot them with bullets, and when bullets hit enemies they explode. This means we'll have dozens of enemy ships, bullets, and explosions all in our window at once. We need a way to deal with tons of sprites in our game—adding them, deleting them, and managing all their interactions.

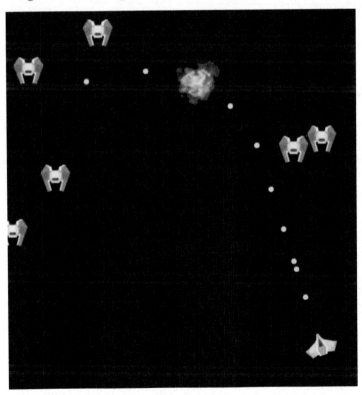

You'll learn how to create and handle all of these sprites with one great tool, the array. An array holds a list of objects, which in this game are sprites. When you need a new sprite, such as a new enemy or bullet, you add it to the array, and when one is destroyed, you remove it. By *iterating* through your arrays, you move and draw all these sprites.

Sector Five starts without any enemies or bullets. Enemies appear at random times and fall from the top, while bullets are created by the player. Once both enemies and bullets are in your window, you check for collisions between them. When a bullet hits an enemy, you remove both and add an explosion. Explosions are a little different from the other sprites. The explosion image is animated, like a little movie that plays within the window.

In this chapter we'll:

- Use arrays to hold many sprites of the same kind.

- Iterate through an array with the each() method to move and draw all the sprites.

- Detect collisions between sprites.

- Create explosion sprites with animated images.

When you're finished, your sprite game toolkit will be getting pretty full. You'll add some finishing touches in the next chapter.

Make More Enemies

Having a single enemy that falls from the top of the window to the bottom was a good way to write and test the Enemy class. Now let's replace that single enemy with a stream of enemies. You can store all the enemies that are in the game using a single Ruby array called @enemies.

The Array class has lots and lots of methods,[1] but you'll use just three of them in Sector Five.

push()   The push() method adds a new object to the array. When it's time to add a new enemy, you write:

```
@enemies.push Enemy.new(self)
```

...and one more enemy is added to the array. It's up to you to make sure you don't add anything to the array that's not an enemy.

delete()   When it's time to remove an enemy, you use the delete() method. If the enemy to remove is stored in the variable enemy_to_remove, you say:

```
@enemies.delete enemy_to_remove
```

...and poof! One fewer enemy.

each()   When you want to do something to *each* of the enemies in the array, such as move them or check to see whether they are touching a bullet, you use the each() method to loop through the enemies:

```
@enemies.each do |enemy|
  #do something to enemy here
end
```

Use the each() method to move your sprites, draw them, and test for collisions between them.

To use an array to hold your enemies, you don't change anything about the Enemy class. You just change how you create, move, and draw enemies in the SectorFive class.

Create an Empty Array

In the initialize() method of the SectorFive class, you wrote one line to create a single enemy:

SectorFive/SectorFive_2/sector_five.rb
```
def initialize
  super(WIDTH,HEIGHT)
  self.caption = 'Sector Five'
  @player = Player.new(self)
➤ @enemy = Enemy.new(self)
end
```

---

1.   You can see all the methods of the Array class by looking in the Ruby documentation at http://ruby-doc.org//core-2.0.0/Array.html.

Now let's replace that line with one that creates an empty array. An array in Ruby can be written as a list of objects separated by commas and surrounded by square brackets. Square brackets with nothing inside denote an empty array:

SectorFive/SectorFive_3/sector_five.rb

```
def initialize
  super(WIDTH, HEIGHT)
  self.caption = 'Sector Five'
  @player = Player.new(self)
➤  @enemies = []
end
```

You add new enemies to the array in the update() method. The initialize() method runs only once, so if you wanted to create your enemies there, you'd have to decide in advance how many to create.

Ruby Refresher: Arrays

Arrays are a key part of Sector Five, and you'll find them very helpful in almost any kind of game you want to write. If you're a little rusty with Ruby arrays, or you learned arrays in another language and could use a little help with Ruby syntax, some of the resources mentioned in Chapter 2, *Get Ready*, on page 5, might give you some help. In particular, Chapter 8 of Chris Pine's book *Learn to Program [Pin09]*, called *Arrays and Iterators*, is a great introduction.

Add a Stream of Enemies

Enemies appear from above and fall down through the window. If you added an enemy every update, your window would be full of enemies. Instead, let's have a small chance of a new enemy appearing each frame. This number helps determine how difficult the game is, and you might want to change it later, so make it a constant of the SectorFive class, called ENEMY_FREQUENCY. Set it initially to 0.05.

SectorFive/SectorFive_3/sector_five.rb

```
class SectorFive < Gosu::Window
  WIDTH = 800
  HEIGHT = 600
➤  ENEMY_FREQUENCY = 0.05
```

In the update() method, create a random number each frame. If that number is less than ENEMY_FREQUENCY, a new enemy is added to the array using the push() method. Put this code at the beginning of the update() method:

SectorFive/SectorFive_3/sector_five.rb

```
def update
  @player.turn_left if button_down?(Gosu::KbLeft)
  @player.turn_right if button_down?(Gosu::KbRight)
  @player.accelerate if button_down?(Gosu::KbUp)
  @player.move
➤ if rand < ENEMY_FREQUENCY
➤   @enemies.push Enemy.new(self)
➤ end
end
```

When used with no argument, the rand() method returns a value between zero and one. If ENEMY_FREQUENCY is 0.05, you add an enemy about one frame in twenty. At sixty frames per second, that's about three enemies per second, which should be enough to cause your player some serious trouble.

Move All the Enemies

When the update() method runs, your @enemies array might have one enemy, or zero enemies, or forty-seven enemies. What you want is for each of them to move down the window. First, in the update() method of SectorFive, remove the single line of code that moved one enemy:

SectorFive/SectorFive_2/sector_five.rb

```
def update
  @player.turn_left if button_down?(Gosu::KbLeft)
  @player.turn_right if button_down?(Gosu::KbRight)
  @player.accelerate if button_down?(Gosu::KbUp)
  @player.move
➤ @enemy.move
end
```

You can replace it with three lines of code that tell each member of the @enemies array to move. You do this with the each() method of the Array class. When you use each(), you create a temporary variable, in this case called enemy.

SectorFive/SectorFive_3/sector_five.rb

```
def update
  @player.turn_left if button_down?(Gosu::KbLeft)
  @player.turn_right if button_down?(Gosu::KbRight)
  @player.accelerate if button_down?(Gosu::KbUp)
  @player.move
  if rand < ENEMY_FREQUENCY
    @enemies.push Enemy.new(self)
  end
➤ @enemies.each do |enemy|
➤   enemy.move
➤ end
end
```

This is a code pattern we'll be using several times in this game. Using the each() method of the Array class, you iterate through the array. Each of the elements of the array gets a turn being enemy, and each has its move() method called.

If there are no enemies, nothing happens. If there are forty enemies, the move() method is called on each one.

Draw All the Enemies

To draw all the enemies, you do pretty much the same thing you did to move all the enemies. In the draw() method of the SectorFive class, remove the single line of code that draws an enemy:

```
SectorFive/SectorFive_2/sector_five.rb
def draw
  @player.draw
➤   @enemy.draw
end
```

Replace that one line with three lines that use the each() method to draw all the enemies:

```
SectorFive/SectorFive_3/sector_five.rb
def draw
  @player.draw
➤   @enemies.each do |enemy|
➤     enemy.draw
➤   end
end
```

When you run the game now, enemies fall from the top of the window to the bottom.

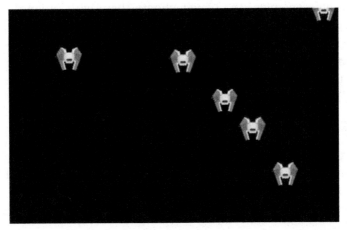

Try adjusting the ENEMY_FREQUENCY constant to see what happens. Make it equal to 1 and see what it looks like if you add an enemy every frame. By changing this number, you can get anything from an occasional enemy to a constant stream. You can't hurt the enemies, so give the player some bullets and let the mayhem begin.

What If It Doesn't Work?

The each() method makes arrays very useful in games, because you don't need to know in advance how many objects are in the array. Errors involving each() will crop up, if only because you use it so often.

The following output was created by replacing enemy.draw with @enemies.draw in the draw() method of the SectorFive class.

```
/Users/mark/Desktop/SectorFive_3/sector_five.rb:54: in `block in draw':
undefined method `draw' for #<Array:0x007fd022803e60> (NoMethodError)
  from /Users/mark/Desktop/SectorFive_3/sector_five.rb:53: in `each'
  from /Users/mark/Desktop/SectorFive_3/sector_five.rb:53: in `draw'
  from /Users/mark/Desktop/SectorFive_3/sector_five.rb:62: in `<main>'
[Finished in 1.5s with exit code 1]
```

The output reminds us that @enemies is an array, not an instance of the Enemy class, and so it doesn't have a draw() method. When you use the each() method to go through the array, the variable enemy becomes each of the elements of the @enemies array in turn, and those elements each have a draw() method.

Fire Bullets

To destroy some enemies, the player shoots them with bullets. Bullets are another kind of sprite, so you can make a class, Bullet, to describe them. When the player presses the spacebar, a bullet will be created. It travels in the direction the ship was pointing when it was fired until it hits an enemy or flies out of the window. When a bullet hits an enemy ship, both are destroyed in a ball of flame.

The Bullet Class

You've already made two sprite classes, so you're probably getting the hang of it. When you make a bullet, you tell it where to start and what direction to go. Once you've made a bullet, it should keep moving in that direction until it hits an enemy or flies out the window. Here is a diagram for the Bullet class:

class Bullet
@window
@x
@y
@direction
@image
@radius
initialize( )
draw( )
move( )

Start by creating a bullet.rb file and saving it in the same folder as sector_five.rb.

When you create a bullet, it has the same position and angle as the player ship at the time the spacebar is pressed. So the initialize() method of the Bullet class takes these values as arguments and then saves them in instance variables:

SectorFive/SectorFive_3/bullet.rb
```
class Bullet
  def initialize(window, x, y, angle)
    @x = x
    @y = y
```

```
    @direction = angle
    @image = Gosu::Image.new('images/bullet.png')
    @radius = 3
    @window = window
  end
end
```

The bullet's speed is a constant, so at the top of the Bullet class, before the initialize() method, let's set it to 5:

SectorFive/SectorFive_3/bullet.rb
```
class Bullet
➤ SPEED = 5
```

Once a bullet is fired, you move it each frame of the game. The move() method of the Bullet class uses the Gosu.offet_x() and Gosu.offset_y() methods to change @x and @y:

SectorFive/SectorFive_3/bullet.rb
```
def move
    @x += Gosu.offset_x(@direction, SPEED)
    @y += Gosu.offset_y(@direction, SPEED)
end
```

In the draw() method of the Bullet class, you make sure the image is centered on @x, @y so it appears in the middle of the ship when you shoot.

SectorFive/SectorFive_3/bullet.rb
```
def draw
  @image.draw(@x - @radius, @y - @radius, 1)
end
```

Run the project now. You won't see any bullets, since you haven't actually made any yet. But if you have errors in the bullet.rb file, Ruby will tell you, and you can fix them before you move on.

Add a Bullet at the Player Location

To use the Bullet class in the game, you need to include the new file in sector_five.rb, right after the files for player and enemy:

SectorFive/SectorFive_3/sector_five.rb
```
require 'gosu'
require_relative 'player'
require_relative 'enemy'
➤ require_relative 'bullet'
```

As you did for the enemies, make an empty array in the initialize() method of the SectorFive class:

SectorFive/SectorFive_3/sector_five.rb

```
def initialize
  super(WIDTH, HEIGHT)
  self.caption = 'Sector Five'
  @player = Player.new(self)
  @enemies = []
➤ @bullets = []
end
```

Because you want one bullet per press of the spacebar, use button_down() to create the bullets. You need to *get* the position and direction of the player ship to create a bullet. Ruby has a helper built in for getting instance variables, attr_reader. At the top of the Player class, add a single line of code:

SectorFive/SectorFive_3/player.rb

```
class Player
  ROTATION_SPEED = 3
  ACCELERATION = 2
  FRICTION = 0.9
➤ attr_reader :x, :y, :angle, :radius
```

This line is a shortcut that creates four methods: x(), y(), angle(), and radius(). Each of these methods returns the value of the appropriate instance variable. You use them in the SectorFive class to create the bullets.

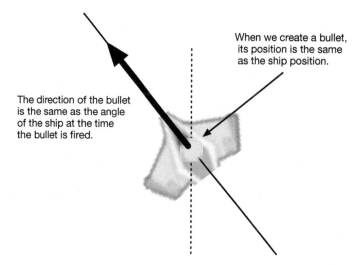

When we create a bullet, its position is the same as the ship position.

The direction of the bullet is the same as the angle of the ship at the time the bullet is fired.

In the button_down(id) method, you create a bullet by passing in the position and angle of the player ship as arguments to the initialize() method. Using button_down(id) means your player gets one bullet per button press and will have to release the spacebar and press it again to get another.

```
SectorFive/SectorFive_3/sector_five.rb
def button_down(id)
    if id == Gosu::KbSpace
      @bullets.push Bullet.new(self, @player.x, @player.y, @player.angle)
    end
end
```

The bullets are created right in the middle of the player ship.

> **Challenge: Move and Draw the Bullets**
>
> Before you go on, see whether you can move and draw all the bullets. All the code
> you add should be in the SectorFive class, in the move() and draw() methods. You have
> enough tools in your toolbox to do it; you already move and draw all the enemies.
> When you're finished, you should be able to run the game and shoot bullets. If you're
> successful, you can skip the next section.

Move and Draw the Bullets

To move the bullets, use the each() method of the array, sending the move()
message to each bullet. Put this in the update() method:

```
SectorFive/SectorFive_3/sector_five.rb
def update
  @player.turn_left if button_down?(Gosu::KbLeft)
  @player.turn_right if button_down?(Gosu::KbRight)
  @player.accelerate if button_down?(Gosu::KbUp)
  @player.move
  if rand < ENEMY_FREQUENCY
    @enemies.push Enemy.new(self)
  end
  @enemies.each do |enemy|
    enemy.move
  end
  @bullets.each do |bullet|
    bullet.move
  end
end
```

To draw the bullets, add the following to the draw() method of the SectorFive
class:

```
SectorFive/SectorFive_3/sector_five.rb
def draw
  @player.draw
  @enemies.each do |enemy|
    enemy.draw
  end
```

```
➤    @bullets.each do |bullet|
➤      bullet.draw
➤    end
end
```

When you run the program now, you can fly around and shoot bullets. The bullets fly in a straight line, right out of the window, passing right through the enemies. We need to fix that.

Handle Collisions

You have a bunch of enemies falling down and bullets moving in all directions. Now you need to know when a bullet hits an enemy. This process of figuring out when two objects touch each other is called *collision detection*.

In Sector Five, we're going to use a very simple algorithm for detecting collisions. We pretend our objects are circular. Our bullets *are* circular, and while our enemies are not precisely circular, they are pretty close. Even if it's not perfect, it will *look* like the enemies explode when our bullets hit them. And that is what we really want.

To figure out whether two circular objects overlap, find the distance between their centers. If that distance is small enough, there is a collision. The threshold distance is the radius of one plus the radius of the other.

distance > enemy.radius + bullet.radius
no collision

distance < enemy.radius + bullet.radius
collision

To check for a collision between one bullet and Whack one enemy, you need to know the position and radius of each. You use the attr_reader helper for this; add a line in the Bullet class, right after the class definition and before the first method:

SectorFive/SectorFive_3/bullet.rb
```
class Bullet
SPEED = 5
➤ attr_reader :x, :y, :radius
```

Then you add the same attr_reader helper to the Enemy class:

SectorFive/SectorFive_3/enemy.rb
```
class Enemy
  SPEED = 4
➤ attr_reader :x, :y, :radius
```

To tell whether any bullets are touching any enemies, you need to check each enemy against each bullet. For instance, if there were twelve bullets and ten enemies in the window, that would be 120 checks. But with the each() method, you can make short work of this task.

This is a little different from using the each() method to move all the enemies or all the bullets. In this case, we plan to *change* the arrays we are iterating through by removing objects from them. To do this, create copies of the arrays with Ruby's dup() method, and then iterate through those. This ensures that each() checks every single bullet and every single enemy.

Start by looping through the enemies. For each enemy, loop through the bullets, again using the each() method. Check all of these combinations to see whether they are touching, and if they are, remove both bullet and enemy.

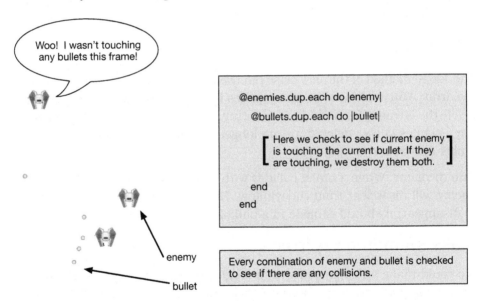

Woo! I wasn't touching any bullets this frame!

```
@enemies.dup.each do |enemy|
  @bullets.dup.each do |bullet|
    [ Here we check to see if current enemy
      is touching the current bullet. If they
      are touching, we destroy them both. ]
  end
end
```

enemy

bullet

Every combination of enemy and bullet is checked to see if there are any collisions.

You use the Gosu.distance() method here, just as you did in Whack-A-Ruby. It calculates the distance between any two points in the scene. When the two objects collide, you delete each from its array. You check for collisions in the update() method of the SectorFive class.

SectorFive/SectorFive_3/sector_five.rb

```
def update
  @player.turn_left if button_down?(Gosu::KbLeft)
  @player.turn_right if button_down?(Gosu::KbRight)
  @player.accelerate if button_down?(Gosu::KbUp)
  @player.move
  if rand < ENEMY_FREQUENCY
    @enemies.push Enemy.new(self)
  end
  @enemies.each do |enemy|
    enemy.move
  end
  @bullets.each do |bullet|
    bullet.move
  end
  @enemies.dup.each do |enemy|
    @bullets.dup.each do |bullet|
      distance = Gosu.distance(enemy.x, enemy.y, bullet.x, bullet.y)
      if distance < enemy.radius + bullet.radius
        @enemies.delete enemy
        @bullets.delete bullet
      end
    end
  end
end
```

The delete() method of the Array class removes the argument of the method from the array. You don't need to erase sprites from the window yourself. You just delete the enemies from the @enemies array. When Gosu calls the draw() method, any enemies you've deleted are no longer in the array, and so they are no longer drawn in the window.

Run the game. When a bullet collides with an enemy, both the bullet and the enemy will disappear from the window. But you don't just want the enemy to disappear; it should explode in a ball of fire.

Make Animated Explosions

We could make an explosion with a single image, but it wouldn't look very convincing. Our explosion starts as a bright yellow ball of flame and then fades away, turning a darker orange and getting smaller. You do this by drawing sixteen images in the same location. When the explosion first appears, you draw the first in the sequence of images. Each subsequent time the game runs the draw() method, the next image in the sequence is drawn.

Use a Sprite Sheet

One way to load your images would be to copy sixteen individual image files into your project and then load them into an array of images. This would work fine, though it might involve a lot of typing. Game artists often group related images together by stitching them into a single image, called a *sprite sheet*. You'll use the following sprite sheet for your explosion animation:

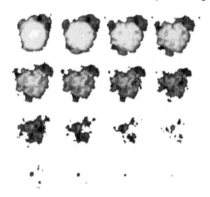

The image at the top left of the sprite sheet is drawn first, and the image at the bottom right is drawn last. You can get tools to help you make a sprite sheet, and you can find sprite sheets online in the same way you can find other game images. Now you can set up your Explosion class to load its images from this sprite sheet.

In a new file called explosion.rb, create the empty Explosion class:

SectorFive/SectorFive_3/explosion.rb
```
class Explosion
end
```

Also import explosion.rb into the sector_five.rb file:

SectorFive/SectorFive_3/sector_five.rb
```
require_relative 'explosion'
```

Instead of a single image, the Explosion class uses an array of images. Other than that, it's much like the other sprite classes. A variable called @image_index keeps track of the current image, while @finished is a Boolean variable you set to true when your little animation is complete. This is shown in the class diagram on page 72.

To make a new explosion, pass in the location as arguments. The @images array gets created using a method of the Gosu::Image class called load_tiles(). This

class Explosion
@window @x @y @images @image_number @finished
initialize( ) draw( )

method chops up the sprite sheet into rectangles and returns an array of images.

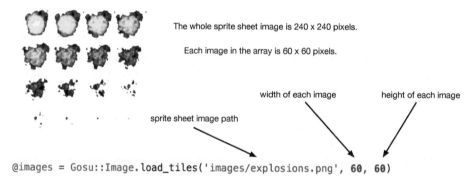

The whole sprite sheet image is 240 x 240 pixels.

Each image in the array is 60 x 60 pixels.

width of each image   height of each image

sprite sheet image path

```
@images = Gosu::Image.load_tiles('images/explosions.png', 60, 60)
```

Here is the initialize() method of the Explosion class:

SectorFive/SectorFive_3/explosion.rb
```
def initialize(window, x, y)
  @x = x
  @y = y
  @radius = 30
  @images = Gosu::Image.load_tiles('images/explosions.png', 60, 60)
  @image_index = 0
  @finished = false
end
```

The Explosion class doesn't need a move() method, since the explosions stay in one place.

Animating the Explosion

Now that you've got sixteen explosion images in the @images array, you need to cycle through them, drawing a different one each frame for sixteen frames. You do it all in the draw() method of the Explosion class.

First, check to see whether the @image_index variable is in the range of the array. If it is, draw the current image and increment @image_index so the next image in the array is drawn in the next frame of the game. If you've run out of images, you don't draw anything and you set the @finished variable to true. Later, you'll check this value and remove finished explosions from the array.

SectorFive/SectorFive_3/explosion.rb
```
def draw
  if @image_index < @images.count  ← undefined method error for this
    @images[@image_index].draw(@x - @radius, @y - @radius, 2)
    @image_index += 1
  else
    @finished = true
  end
end
```

Array numbering starts at zero, so the highest number of the index of the array is one less than the count. If there are sixteen images in the array, @image_index goes from zero up to fifteen. If you tried to draw number sixteen, you'd get an error and crash your game.

Note that you cannot just use each() to draw all the explosion images. If you tried, Gosu would draw all the explosion images during a single run of the draw() method. Instead of an animation, all the images would appear at once, and only for a single frame. To spread out drawing the images over sixteen frames of the game, you need to manage the images yourself, keeping track of which one you're drawing in each frame.

Make Them Explode

You've written the Explosion class, and now you're ready to use it to make some enemies explode. First, add a line of code in the initialize() method of the SectorFive class to create an empty array where you can put the explosions, just like you already do for bullets and enemies:

SectorFive/SectorFive_3/sector_five.rb
```
def initialize
  super(WIDTH, HEIGHT)
  self.caption = 'Sector Five'
  @player = Player.new(self)
  @enemies = []
```

```
    @bullets = []
➤    @explosions = []
  end
```

You're already checking for collisions between bullets and enemies, and removing the enemies. In that same loop, you also create a new explosion and add it to the array:

SectorFive/SectorFive_3/sector_five.rb
```
def update
  @player.turn_left if button_down?(Gosu::KbLeft)
  @player.turn_right if button_down?(Gosu::KbRight)
  @player.accelerate if button_down?(Gosu::KbUp)
  @player.move
  if rand < ENEMY_FREQUENCY
    @enemies.push Enemy.new(self)
  end
  @enemies.each do |enemy|
    enemy.move
  end
  @bullets.each do |bullet|
    bullet.move
  end
  @enemies.dup.each do |enemy|
    @bullets.dup.each do |bullet|
      distance = Gosu.distance(enemy.x, enemy.y, bullet.x, bullet.y)
      if distance < enemy.radius + bullet.radius
        @enemies.delete enemy
        @bullets.delete bullet
➤        @explosions.push Explosion.new(self, enemy.x, enemy.y)
      end
    end
  end
end
```

Note that only the highlighted line of code is new. In the draw() method of the SectorFive class, you add a loop to draw the explosions:

SectorFive/SectorFive_3/sector_five.rb
```
def draw
  @player.draw
  @enemies.each do |enemy|
    enemy.draw
  end
  @bullets.each do |bullet|
    bullet.draw
  end
➤  @explosions.each do |explosion|
➤    explosion.draw
➤  end
end
```

When you run the program now and you shoot some enemies, they explode. So we're finished, right?

Play for a while. You might notice that the game starts to slow down. This might happen fairly quickly, or it might take a while, depending on your computer. But eventually the game will *really* slow down. Our arrays are getting too big, and the computer is taking too long to do all the calculations for each frame.

Cleaning Up Your Arrays

You've added a whole bunch of sprites to your arrays—enemies, bullets, and explosions. You have deleted a few enemies and bullets that collided, but many enemies and bullets simply fly off the sides of your game and disappear. They may be gone from the window, but they are still in your arrays. And all the explosions are still hanging around, even though they aren't being drawn. So our arrays start to get really big, and we're still using the each() method to move and draw them. Ruby is doing a lot of calculations to move sprites you can't even see. You can fix this by deleting the sprites you're no longer using.

Delete the Explosions

Right now, each explosion stops drawing itself after its sixteen frames of images, but it is still there, cluttering up your @explosions array. The solution is to delete the explosion when you're finished with it. That's what the @finished variable is for. In the initialize() method of the Explosion class, set @finished to false. In the draw() method, set it to true when @image_index gets beyond the range of the @images array.

To remove the explosions that are finished, in the update() method you can check all of your explosions and remove any whose @finished variable has been set to true. So you can ask if an explosion is finished, you use the attr_reader helper in the Explosion class:

SectorFive/SectorFive_3/explosion.rb
```
class Explosion
➤   attr_reader :finished
```

Then you remove the expired explosions by adding to the update() method of the SectorFive class. Use the dup() method on the array, since you're changing the array as you iterate through it:

SectorFive/SectorFive_3/sector_five.rb
```
def update
  @player.turn_left if button_down?(Gosu::KbLeft)
  @player.turn_right if button_down?(Gosu::KbRight)
```

```
  @player.accelerate if button_down?(Gosu::KbUp)
  @player.move
  if rand < ENEMY_FREQUENCY
    @enemies.push Enemy.new(self)
  end
  @enemies.each do |enemy|
    enemy.move
  end
  @bullets.each do |bullet|
    bullet.move
  end
  @enemies.dup.each do |enemy|
    @bullets.dup.each do |bullet|
      distance = Gosu.distance(enemy.x, enemy.y, bullet.x, bullet.y)
      if distance < enemy.radius + bullet.radius
        @enemies.delete enemy
        @bullets.delete bullet
        @explosions.push Explosion.new(self, enemy.x, enemy.y)
      end
    end
  end
➤ @explosions.dup.each do |explosion|
➤   @explosions.delete explosion if explosion.finished
➤ end
end
```

Now only the explosions you can see are still in the @explosions array.

Delete Bullets and Enemies

You can remove enemies and bullets from your arrays when they are no longer visible in the window. Enemies just fall off the bottom, while the bullets can exit from any side of the window. The test for enemies is simple enough that you can put it right in the update() method. The test to see whether bullets are still in the window is more complicated, and you'll move the code to the Bullet class so you can keep your update() method as simple as possible.

Give the Bullet class a new method, named onscreen?(). This method returns true if the position of the bullet is within the bounds of the window, and false if it is not.

The last line of onscreen?() is true only if the bullet is between the left and right edges, and also between the top and bottom:

SectorFive/SectorFive_3/bullet.rb
```
def onscreen?
  right = @window.width + @radius
  left = -@radius
  top = -@radius
```

```
  bottom = @window.height + @radius
  @x > left and @x < right and @y > top and @y < bottom
end
```

In the update() method, loop through the bullets and remove the ones that are no longer in the window:

SectorFive/SectorFive_3/sector_five.rb
```
def update
  @player.turn_left if button_down?(Gosu::KbLeft)
  @player.turn_right if button_down?(Gosu::KbRight)
  @player.accelerate if button_down?(Gosu::KbUp)
  @player.move
  if rand < ENEMY_FREQUENCY
    @enemies.push Enemy.new(self)
  end
  @enemies.each do |enemy|
    enemy.move
  end
  @bullets.each do |bullet|
    bullet.move
  end
  @enemies.dup.each do |enemy|
    @bullets.dup.each do |bullet|
      distance = Gosu.distance(enemy.x, enemy.y, bullet.x, bullet.y)
      if distance < enemy.radius + bullet.radius
        @enemies.delete enemy
        @bullets.delete bullet
        @explosions.push Explosion.new(self, enemy.x, enemy.y)
      end
    end
  end
  @explosions.dup.each do |explosion|
    @explosions.delete explosion if explosion.finished
  end
➤  @enemies.dup.each do |enemy|
➤    if enemy.y > HEIGHT + enemy.radius
➤      @enemies.delete enemy
➤    end
➤  end
➤  @bullets.dup.each do |bullet|
➤    @bullets.delete bullet unless bullet.onscreen?
➤  end
end
```

Now you can play for a long time, and the game won't slow down. The arrays only have the objects that you see in the window, so they never grow out of control.

Make It Your Own

At this point, you have an almost complete sprite-based game. This is a good point to stop and make some changes. Trying some experiments with the game will hone your skills and prepare you to bring some of your own game ideas to life. Here are a few ideas for changes you could make. Save a copy of your game before you start.

Make explosions drift.

Make the explosions drift. In a random direction, or down, or whatever you like. You need to give the Explosion class a move() method and call that method on all the explosions.

Make explosions kill enemies.

Make the explosions collide with enemies, destroying the enemies if they are too close to the explosions. You need to test, just as you did with bullets and enemies, whether any of the explosions are close enough to enemies to make them explode. See whether you can get some explosion chain reactions going.

Make enemies fall at different speeds.

Right now, the Enemy class has a constant SPEED, but you could change it to an instance variable, and set it to a random number in initialize().

Slow down the explosion animation.

Make each image in the animation last for two or three frames in the game. There are several ways to accomplish this. One would be to make a separate @frame_count variable and then calculate @image_count from that.

Have the enemies shoot at the player.

This is a big change and a significant challenge. Use the Bullet class if you can, rather than making a new class. Maybe add an instance variable that keeps track of whose bullet it is, and use a different image depending on whether it's a player bullet or an enemy bullet. You could have the enemies fire randomly or in the direction of the player.

What's Next

Your sprite game toolkit is getting pretty full. You have only a few types of sprites, but you can make as many of each kind as you need. You can detect and handle key presses and collisions. Next, you'll finish your game by adding multiple *scenes*, so that you can give the player some instructions at the beginning and a score at the end. You'll also add background music and sound effects to add depth to your game.

CHAPTER 6

Adding Scenes and Sounds

Our game now has lots of sprites and is pretty fun to play. In its current state, it's more the *core* of a game than it is an actual game. Imagine if we shared our game with some friends. They might have no idea what to do, which keys to press, or even that the falling ships are enemies that they can shoot. The game also never ends or has any kind of score.

In this chapter we'll change the game to show the players a little information about how to play and let them start the game when they are ready.

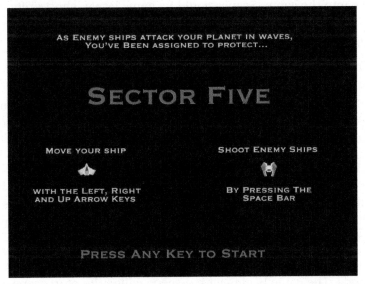

When players press a key, the game itself begins, with enemies descending from the top of the window. The game ends when the player ship touches an enemy or flies off the top, or after one hundred enemy ships have been added. When the game ends, we show players another screen that tells them how they did, with some credits and a choice to play again or quit. Different things are shown in the window before the game begins, during the game, and after it ends. We call these phases of the game *scenes*.

Then we finish up the game by adding music and sounds. A different musical track plays in each scene, helping us establish the proper mood of anticipation, exciting action, or completion. We add some sound effects when enemies explode and when bullets are fired, to bring the player deeper into the game.

In this chapter we'll:

- Create distinct scenes for our game.

- Transition between the scenes.

- Draw scrolling credits on the screen.

- Add sound effects and background music to scenes.

When we're finished, our game will be complete, and we'll be ready to refine it, share it with our friends, and make more games.

Start Over with Scenes

Breaking a game into scenes is a flexible way to incorporate all kinds of mechanics into the game. Scenes could be game levels, short animations, or rooms in a dungeon. They help break a complex game into manageable chunks, like separate mini games that you can build one at a time.

To organize your game into scenes, you'll write a completely new SectorFive class, but in it you'll reuse much of the code from the old one. You won't change your sprite classes at all. In the new SectorFive class, you'll create separate update and draw methods for each scene. Most of the code you wrote in the past few chapters goes into the methods for the *game* scene.

Because you're starting over, you'll make a new file for your new SectorFive class. Create a file called sector_five_scenes.rb and save it in the same folder as sector_five.rb. You're still using all your sprite classes and images, so it's important to save the new file in the same folder as the old one. Don't delete sector_five.rb; you'll be reusing much of its code in the new class.

In the game code, you give your scenes names you'll use in the names of some new methods. The game begins with a scene called the *start* scene and then transitions to the *game* scene when the player presses a key. The game can end in several ways, and when it does, it changes to the *end* scene.

 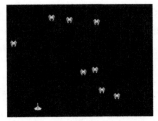 

Breaking the game into scenes changes where you put your code. Each scene gets its own update() and draw() methods. For the start scene, call these methods update_start() and draw_start(), and stick to that naming strategy for your other scenes. When you transition to a new scene, call an initialize method for that scene. For instance, when you want to change to the game scene, call the initialize_game() method. The following figure shows the flow of the three-scene game, with the dotted lines representing the transitions between scenes.

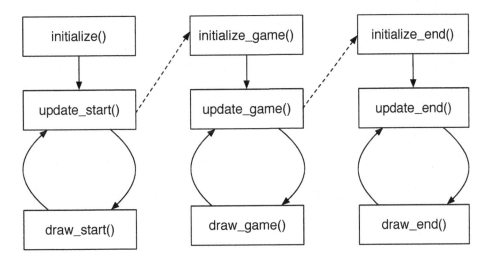

Your task is to achieve the flow in the preceding image with the tools Gosu gives you. Gosu runs the initialize() method, followed by draw() and update() in a loop, as shown in the example in out first game on page 24. To achieve the new flow, you create a variable, @scene, to keep track of the scene you're currently in. Then, in the update() and draw() methods of the SectorFive class, you check to see what scene you're in and run the appropriate method. When you run the transition methods, such as the initialize_game() method, you set up instance variables for the new scene and change the value of @scene so that the appropriate methods are called when Gosu runs its update() and draw() methods.

In the initialize() method, the variable @scene is set to :start. Here is the new Sec-torFive class with its initialize() method:

```
SectorFive/SectorFive_4/sector_five_scenes.rb
require 'gosu'
require_relative 'player'
require_relative 'enemy'
require_relative 'bullet'
require_relative 'explosion'
class SectorFive < Gosu::Window
  WIDTH = 800
  HEIGHT = 600
  ENEMY_FREQUENCY = 0.05
  def initialize
    super(WIDTH, HEIGHT)
    self.caption = "Sector Five"
    @background_image = Gosu::Image.new('images/start_screen.png')
    @scene = :start
  end
end
window = SectorFive.new
window.show
```

You don't need an initialize_start() method, because the initialize() method takes care of setting up the start scene.

Scene Methods

In the draw() method, check the value of @scene and run the appropriate method:

```
SectorFive/SectorFive_4/sector_five_scenes.rb
def draw
  case @scene
  when :start
    draw_start
  when :game
    draw_game
  when :end
    draw_end
  end
end
```

The case control statement makes for readable code and makes it easy to add new scenes later.

Each of the draw methods you've made—draw_start(), draw_game(), and draw_end()—is just like the draw() method before you introduced scenes. In draw_start(), you just draw the background image:

```
SectorFive/SectorFive_4/sector_five_scenes.rb
def draw_start
```

```
      @background_image.draw(0,0,0)
end
```

In the draw_game() method, you can reuse the code that used to be in draw().
You can copy the code from sector_five.rb:

SectorFive/SectorFive_4/sector_five_scenes.rb
```
def draw_game
  @player.draw
  @enemies.each do |enemy|
    enemy.draw
  end
  @bullets.each do |bullet|
    bullet.draw
  end
  @explosions.each do |explosion|
    explosion.draw
  end
end
```

You'll add the draw_end() method later in the chapter, since what you draw
depends on how the game ends.

You'll create your update methods in much the same way. Since you're just
showing a static image in the start scene, you don't actually need an
update_start() method. In the update() method, you check for the other two scenes,
and if @scene is equal to :start, nothing happens:

SectorFive/SectorFive_4/sector_five_scenes.rb
```
def update
  case @scene
  when :game
    update_game
  when :end
    update_end
  end
end
```

When you run the game now, it shows the start scene image. Nothing happens
now until the player presses a key.

Change Scenes

While you're in the start scene, you're waiting for the player to press a key.
You detect the key press using the button_down() method. The button_down() method
does different things depending on which scene you're in, and you don't want
the game to restart every time a key is pressed. Each scene gets a separate
button_down() method, much like it gets its own draw() and update() methods:

```
SectorFive/SectorFive_4/sector_five_scenes.rb
def button_down(id)
  case @scene
  when :start
    button_down_start(id)
  when :game
    button_down_game(id)
  when :end
    button_down_end(id)
  end
end
```

When you are in the start scene and press any key, you transition to the game scene. In button_down_start(), you don't need to check which key was pressed, since you don't really care. You just run the initialize_game() method:

```
SectorFive/SectorFive_4/sector_five_scenes.rb
def button_down_start(id)
  initialize_game
end
```

The initialize_game() method does most of what the initialize() method did in the previous version of the game. You can copy most of it over. Don't run the super() method again, though. The superclass of SectorFive, Gosu::Window, doesn't have an initialize_game() method, so sending that message would cause an error. You also don't need to set the window caption again:

```
SectorFive/SectorFive_4/sector_five_scenes.rb
def initialize_game
  @player = Player.new(self)
  @enemies = []
  @bullets = []
  @explosions = []
  @scene = :game
end
```

In addition to the code you copied from your old initialize(), you've changed the @scene variable to :game. By doing this, you switch from running the update_start() and draw_start() methods in a loop to running the update_game() and draw_game() methods.

Since the game scene is really just the game you wrote before, the update_game() method is what used to be the update() method. You can copy it over exactly, though later you'll add some code to end the game:

```
SectorFive/SectorFive_4/sector_five_scenes.rb
def update_game
  @player.turn_left if button_down?(Gosu::KbLeft)
  @player.turn_right if button_down?(Gosu::KbRight)
```

```
@player.accelerate if button_down?(Gosu::KbUp)
@player.move
if rand < ENEMY_FREQUENCY
  @enemies.push Enemy.new(self)
end
@enemies.each do |enemy|
  enemy.move
end
@bullets.each do |bullet|
  bullet.move
end
@enemies.dup.each do |enemy|
  @bullets.dup.each do |bullet|
    distance = Gosu.distance(enemy.x, enemy.y, bullet.x, bullet.y)
    if distance < enemy.radius + bullet.radius
      @enemies.delete enemy
      @bullets.delete bullet
      @explosions.push Explosion.new(self, enemy.x, enemy.y)
    end
  end
end
@explosions.dup.each do |explosion|
  @explosions.delete explosion if explosion.finished
end
@enemies.dup.each do |enemy|
  if enemy.y > HEIGHT + enemy.radius
    @enemies.delete enemy
  end
end
@bullets.dup.each do |bullet|
  @bullets.delete bullet unless bullet.onscreen?
end
end
```

The code that was in the button_down() method now goes in the button_down_game() method:

SectorFive/SectorFive_4/sector_five_scenes.rb
```
def button_down_game(id)
  if id == Gosu::KbSpace
    @bullets.push Bullet.new(self,  @player.x, @player.y, @player.angle)
  end
end
```

Run the game now and press any key. You've got two scenes. The game is the same as before. There's one more scene to add, for when the game is over. Before you add this scene, though, we need to discuss how the game ends.

End the Game

In some games, the point is to finish some task or get to the highest level. In other games, there is a score that the player can try to beat the next time he or she plays. Our game includes both kinds of goals. The player is rewarded for surviving long enough for one hundred enemies to appear, and at the same time the game counts how many enemies the player destroys. Our game ends in one of three ways:

- One hundred enemy ships have appeared. Yay! The player has survived the wave of enemies.

- An enemy ship has hit the player ship. The player ship is destroyed, but hopefully blew up some enemies first.

- The player ship flew out of the top of the window. The enemy mother ship has destroyed the player ship.

However the game ends, it transitions to the end scene. We display a message telling the player how the game ended and how well he or she did. The end scene is an important part of the game. Its purpose is to let the player play again easily, and it should also provide a way to quit the game gracefully. It's a good place to give credit where credit is due, to the artists who made the graphics and sounds for the game, as well as to the programmer who wrote such an amazing game.

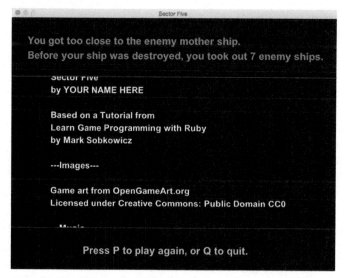

Credits scroll from the bottom to the top of a box inside the window and then repeat.

Keeping Score

Instead of a single score, we keep track of several things during the game. We count how many enemies have appeared and how many enemies the player has destroyed. Let's add some new instance variables for these in the initialize_game() method:

SectorFive/SectorFive_4/sector_five_scenes.rb
```ruby
def initialize_game
  @player = Player.new(self)
  @enemies = []
  @bullets = []
  @explosions = []
  @scene = :game
➤ @enemies_appeared = 0
➤ @enemies_destroyed = 0
end
```

You increment each of these variables in a different place in the program. In each case, you've already written a conditional statement to check for the appropriate event, and you just need to add a statement to change the variable. For @enemies_appeared, you add one to its value in the same place you create enemies—in the update_game() method. Note that the whole update_game() method is not shown, only the code near where you make the addition:

SectorFive/SectorFive_4/sector_five_scenes.rb
```ruby
if rand < ENEMY_FREQUENCY
  @enemies.push Enemy.new(self)
➤ @enemies_appeared += 1
end
```

In the case of @enemies_destroyed, you have a statement in the update_game() method where you do your collision detection. When a bullet hits an enemy, you remove the bullet and the enemy, and add a new explosion. You also increment @enemies_destroyed here:

SectorFive/SectorFive_4/sector_five_scenes.rb
```ruby
@enemies.dup.each do |enemy|
  @bullets.dup.each do |bullet|
    distance = Gosu.distance(enemy.x, enemy.y, bullet.x, bullet.y)
    if distance < enemy.radius + bullet.radius
      @enemies.delete enemy
      @bullets.delete bullet
      @explosions.push Explosion.new(self, enemy.x, enemy.y)
➤     @enemies_destroyed += 1
    end
  end
end
```

However the game ends, you call the initialize_end() method and pass in a single argument that describes how the game ended. You'll write that method a little later; for now you just need to know that it takes that one argument.

One way the game can end is if enough enemies have appeared. You name the maximum number of enemies MAX_ENEMIES and set it to 100 in the same place you create your other constants:

SectorFive/SectorFive_4/sector_five_scenes.rb
```
class SectorFive < Gosu::Window
  WIDTH = 800
  HEIGHT = 600
  ENEMY_FREQUENCY = 0.05
➤  MAX_ENEMIES = 100
```

In the update_game() method, you check each of your endgame conditions. If any is fulfilled, you call the initialize_end() method with the appropriate argument.

First you check whether the number of enemies that has appeared exceeds the value of MAX_ENEMIES. If it does, you call the initialize_end() method with :count_reached as the argument.

To end the game when an enemy ship collides with the player, you loop through the enemy ships to see whether an enemy hits the player ship. If one does, you call the initialize_end() method with the argument :hit_by_enemy.

This code is similar to what you wrote to check for collisions between bullets and enemies; the difference is that there is only one player instance, @player, so you only loop through the @enemies array and check each one to see whether it has collided with the player ship.

If the player ship flies off the top of the screen, it comes in range of the enemy mother ship and is instantly destroyed. In this case you send the argument :off_top. Your update_game() method now looks like the following; the new code is highlighted at the bottom:

SectorFive/SectorFive_4/sector_five_scenes.rb
```
def update_game
  @player.turn_left if button_down?(Gosu::KbLeft)
  @player.turn_right if button_down?(Gosu::KbRight)
  @player.accelerate if button_down?(Gosu::KbUp)
  @player.move
  if rand < ENEMY_FREQUENCY
    @enemies.push Enemy.new(self)
    @enemies_appeared += 1
  end
  @enemies.each do |enemy|
    enemy.move
```

```
      end
      @bullets.each do |bullet|
        bullet.move
      end
      @enemies.dup.each do |enemy|
        @bullets.dup.each do |bullet|
          distance = Gosu.distance(enemy.x, enemy.y, bullet.x, bullet.y)
          if distance < enemy.radius + bullet.radius
            @enemies.delete enemy
            @bullets.delete bullet
            @explosions.push Explosion.new(self, enemy.x, enemy.y)
            @enemies_destroyed += 1
          end
        end
      end
      @explosions.dup.each do |explosion|
        @explosions.delete explosion if explosion.finished
      end
      @enemies.dup.each do |enemy|
        if enemy.y > HEIGHT + enemy.radius
          @enemies.delete enemy
        end
      end
      @bullets.dup.each do |bullet|
        @bullets.delete bullet unless bullet.onscreen?
      end
➤     initialize_end(:count_reached) if @enemies_appeared > MAX_ENEMIES
➤     @enemies.each do |enemy|
➤       distance = Gosu.distance(enemy.x, enemy.y, @player.x, @player.y)
➤       initialize_end(:hit_by_enemy) if distance < @player.radius + enemy.radius
➤     end
➤     initialize_end(:off_top) if @player.y < -@player.radius
      end
```

However the game ends, you don't just want to quit, you want to tell players how they did and encourage them to try again.

Scrolling Credits

Making your credits scroll up the window lets you fit any amount of text into a finite space. Because you want to give credit to everyone who created the art and music for your game, not to mention the programmer, you end up with too much text to fit into the window at once. Plus, scrolling credits look both classic and cool.

Gosu makes it easy to write text on one line, but if you want multiple lines of text, you need to take care of it yourself, by drawing each line separately. To make your credits scroll up the window, use a strategy similar to the one you used to make enemies fall from the top. In your end scene, the credits will scroll up between horizontal red lines, while the text at the top and bottom of the window stays fixed.

Each line of text will be treated as a sprite, which you initially place below the bottom of the window. In the update_end() method, you move each credit up in the window. When the last line gets above the top of the window, you move all the lines back to their starting positions, and the process starts over.

Start by creating a Credit class in a new file, credit.rb. Make the speed of the credits a constant, equal to 1. The initialize() method takes a string value that is the text you want to display on one line, along with x and y values for the initial position of the credit. The initial y position of the credit is stored in a separate variable, so you can reset your credits and run them again after they've finished:

SectorFive/SectorFive_4/credit.rb

```
class Credit
  SPEED = 1
  attr_reader :y

  def initialize(window, text, x, y)
    @x = x
    @y = @initial_y = y
    @text = text
    @font = Gosu::Font.new(24)
  end
end
```

The Credit class needs move() and draw() methods, much like those in the Enemies class. In addition, make a reset() method, so you can start your credits over:

SectorFive/SectorFive_4/credit.rb
```
def move
  @y -= SPEED
end

def draw
  @font.draw(@text, @x, @y, 1)
end

def reset
  @y = @initial_y
end
```

To use the Credit class in your game, require it along with our other classes:

SectorFive/SectorFive_4/sector_five_scenes.rb
```
require 'gosu'
require_relative 'player'
require_relative 'enemy'
require_relative 'bullet'
require_relative 'explosion'
➤ require_relative 'credit'
```

The initialize_end() method sets up the end scene. In it, you create an instance of Gosu::Font to draw your end message on the screen, and create and fill your array of credits.

You create three lines of messages that won't move up the screen. Two of these, @message and @message2, will be at the top and depend on how the game ended. The third, @bottom_message, always says the same thing.

You could load up the credits by writing a line of code for each credit, but instead, load them from a text file. Then, you can change the credits any time by editing the file. Start with the following text in the credits.txt file:

```
Sector Five
by YOUR NAME HERE

Based on a Tutorial from
Learn Game Programming with Ruby
by Mark Sobkowicz

---Images---

Game art from OpenGameArt.org
Licensed under Creative Commons: Public Domain CC0
```

Create one credit from each line of the text file. If you leave a blank line, a blank credit is created, which leaves a gap between the lines of text. Create the first credit at y = 700, near the bottom of the screen. Each one after has a y that is 30 more than the one before. This makes the credits appear in a list. Some of the credits are initially below the bottom of the screen, but that's fine. You scroll them up the screen in update_end():

SectorFive/SectorFive_4/sector_five_scenes.rb

```
def initialize_end(fate)
  case fate
  when :count_reached
    @message = "You made it!  You destroyed #{@enemies_destroyed} ships"
    @message2= "and #{100 - @enemies_destroyed} reached the base."
  when :hit_by_enemy
    @message = "You were struck by an enemy ship."
    @message2 = "Before your ship was destroyed, "
    @message2 += "you took out #{@enemies_destroyed} enemy ships."
  when :off_top
    @message = "You got too close to the enemy mother ship."
    @message2 = "Before your ship was destroyed, "
    @message2 += "you took out #{@enemies_destroyed} enemy ships."
  end
  @bottom_message = "Press P to play again, or Q to quit."
  @message_font = Gosu::Font.new(28)
  @credits = []
  y = 700
  File.open('credits.txt').each do |line|
    @credits.push(Credit.new(self,line.chomp,100,y))
    y+=30
  end
  @scene = :end
end
```

When text is loaded line by line from a file, each line of text has a line break at the end. Gosu::Font throws an error if you try to draw text with a line break, so you can use the chomp() method to remove the breaks.

In the draw_end() method, you want the credits to be drawn only within an invisible box on the screen, as if there were a window over part of the screen through which you could see the credits. To do this, Gosu::Window has a clip_to() method, which takes four arguments. The first two are the x and y position of the top-left corner of a rectangle, and the second two are the width and height of the rectangle. You also draw your messages and red lines at the top and bottom of the scrolling credits region:

SectorFive/SectorFive_4/sector_five_scenes.rb
```
def draw_end
  clip_to(50,140,700,360) do
    @credits.each do |credit|
      credit.draw
    end
  end
  draw_line(0,140,Gosu::Color::RED,WIDTH,140,Gosu::Color::RED)
  @message_font.draw(@message,40,40,1,1,1,Gosu::Color::FUCHSIA)
  @message_font.draw(@message2,40,75,1,1,1,Gosu::Color::FUCHSIA)
  draw_line(0,500,Gosu::Color::RED,WIDTH,500,Gosu::Color::RED)
  @message_font.draw(@bottom_message,180,540,1,1,1,Gosu::Color::AQUA)
end
```

The top and bottom messages are drawn in color. The color is an optional argument to the Gosu::Font.draw() method, and to use it you need to include two more optional arguments before the color, which are x and y scaling factors. Use the color constants Gosu::Color::RED, Gosu::Color::AQUA, and Gosu::Color::FUCHSIA. Don't worry if you haven't heard of fuchsia; you can look up the color constants in the Gosu documentation.[1]

In the update_end() method, move the credits, and when they get high enough on the screen so that the bottom credit is no longer visible, reset them to their original positions and watch them go by again. Because your clipping rectangle starts at y = 300, you reset them when the last credit reaches y = 250:

SectorFive/SectorFive_4/sector_five_scenes.rb
```
def update_end
  @credits.each do |credit|
    credit.move
  end
  if @credits.last.y < 150
    @credits.each do |credit|
      credit.reset
    end
  end
end
```

There are many things you could adjust here, including placement and size of text, colors, and the speed of the credits. Go ahead: change them to your liking.

Play Again

When you're in the end scene, give the player the choice of quitting or playing again. If the player chooses to play again, you need to make sure all the correct

---

1. http://www.libgosu.org/rdoc/Gosu/Color.html

variables are reset. To do this, you can just run the initialize_game() method, which sets up a new game. Make the transition in button_down_end():

```
SectorFive/SectorFive_4/sector_five_scenes.rb
def button_down_end(id)
  if id == Gosu::KbP
    initialize_game
  elsif id == Gosu::KbQ
    close
  end
end
```

We're getting very close. The game is eerily quiet, though, which we need to fix before the game is complete.

Add Music and Sounds

Music and sounds help set a mood, add another dimension to your game, and make your game more polished. Let's add a different background track to each scene and add sound effects for shooting and explosions. Gosu makes a distinction between background music, which plays for a long time, and sound effects, which are short. Background music is streamed, so the entire file does not need to be loaded into memory and is not synchronized with the game. Sound effects, or *samples*, are loaded into memory so that they can play at exactly the right moment in your game. It wouldn't do to have a lag between the enemy exploding and the explosion sound.

Finding Sounds

What you need are electronic files of sounds in WAV or OGG format. If you have files in MP3 or some other format, they might work; you can try it. But WAV and OGG files should work across all platforms, so if you want to distribute your game to other people, you should find files in one of these formats, or convert the files you have into one of these formats.

Playing sounds with Gosu can be troublesome, and if you look through the Gosu forums, this seems to be a pain point for many Gosu programmers. As you work with Gosu, you may have various sounds or songs either refuse to play or play badly. The first thing to try is using a different sound format. OGG files seem to work the most consistently across all platforms, but WAV files may work better on your computer. To convert sounds, you can try the MediaHuman Audio Converter,[2] which is free for OS X and Windows. The code included with this book includes sound files in OGG format.

---

2. http://www.mediahuman.com/audio-converter/

You can make these files yourself or find them online, much like images. Perhaps you know someone who makes music and would like one of his or her songs immortalized in your game. Or maybe you're a musician yourself. But if not, there are many sources of music online. Several are listed in *Images and Sounds*, on page 181.

Add Background Music

Two of the songs included in the tutorial are written by Kevin MacLeod and published on his website, incompetech.com. The third is by Tanner Helland and is published at tannerhelland.com. They are released under Creative Commons licenses, which allows us to use them in any project, including a commercial project. We need to give credit to the creator, which we do by including the following text in the credits.txt file:

```
---Music---

"Lost Frontier" Kevin MacLeod (incompetech.com)
"Cephalopod" Kevin MacLeod (incompetech.com)
Licensed under Creative Commons: By Attribution 3.0
http://creativecommons.org/licenses/by/3.0/

"From Here" Tanner Helland (tannerhelland.com)
Licensed under Creative Commons: Attribution-ShareAlike 3.0
http://creativecommons.org/licenses/by-sa/3.0/
```

The three songs are for the start, game, and end scenes. For each song, you create an instance of Gosu::Song, which takes only a file path as an argument. Then play the song with the play() method. In the initialize() method of SectorFive, add and play the first song:

```
SectorFive/SectorFive_4/sector_five_scenes.rb
def initialize
  super(WIDTH, HEIGHT)
  self.caption = "Sector Five"
  @background_image = Gosu::Image.new('images/start_screen.png')
  @scene = :start
➤ @start_music = Gosu::Song.new('sounds/Lost Frontier.ogg')
➤ @start_music.play(true)
end
```

Passing the optional value true to the play() method plays the song in a loop, so that if the song reaches the end, it starts over. Some songs made for video games are designed to loop in such a way that you can't tell when it starts over. In the initialize_game() method, you can add and play the next song. This one plays while the player shoots the ships, so it's fast-paced and energetic:

SectorFive/SectorFive_4/sector_five_scenes.rb

```ruby
def initialize_game
  @player = Player.new(self)
  @enemies = []
  @bullets = []
  @explosions = []
  @scene = :game
  @enemies_appeared = 0
  @enemies_destroyed = 0
➤ @game_music = Gosu::Song.new('sounds/Cephalopod.ogg')
➤ @game_music.play(true)
end
```

You don't need to end the first song. Gosu plays only one song at a time, so starting a new song stops whatever song was playing before.

In the initialize_end() method, load and play the third song:

SectorFive/SectorFive_4/sector_five_scenes.rb

```ruby
def initialize_end(fate)
  case fate
  when :count_reached
    @message = "You made it!  You destroyed #{@enemies_destroyed} ships"
    @message2= "and #{100 - @enemies_destroyed} reached the base."
  when :hit_by_enemy
    @message = "You were struck by an enemy ship."
    @message2 = "Before your ship was destroyed, "
    @message2 += "you took out #{@enemies_destroyed} enemy ships."
  when :off_top
    @message = "You got too close to the enemy mother ship."
    @message2 = "Before your ship was destroyed, "
    @message2 += "you took out #{@enemies_destroyed} enemy ships."
  end
  @bottom_message = "Press P to play again, or Q to quit."
  @message_font = Gosu::Font.new(28)
  @credits = []
  y = 700
  File.open('credits.txt').each do |line|
    @credits.push(Credit.new(self,line.chomp,100,y))
    y+=30
  end
  @scene = :end
➤ @end_music = Gosu::Song.new('sounds/FromHere.ogg')
➤ @end_music.play(true)
end
```

When you play your game now, music plays throughout—moody background music at the beginning and end, and thumping action music while the actual game is running. Next we need to hear those explosions.

Add Sound Effects

While music adds to the overall mood and experience of a game, sound effects provide feedback and improve the feeling of immersion in the world you've created. Animated fireballs are good, but animated fireballs accompanied by booming explosion sounds are better.

Gosu provides another class for short sounds that play when actions occur in the game. The Gosu::Sample class stores sound files in memory and plays them on demand. They play over the music—and over each other—so it's best not to make them too long. The two sound effects included in this tutorial are each less than one second long. One, explosion.ogg, is for when enemies explode, and the other, shoot.ogg, is for each time we shoot a bullet. These sound files are from the freesound.org website and have been placed in the public domain. Add this information to the credits file:

```
---Sound Effects---

Sound effects from freesound.org
Licensed under Creative Commons: Public Domain CC0
```

Load the sounds in the initialize_game() method. Then they'll be ready to play when you need them.

SectorFive/SectorFive_4/sector_five_scenes.rb
```
def initialize_game
  @player = Player.new(self)
  @enemies = []
  @bullets = []
  @explosions = []
  @scene = :game
  @enemies_appeared = 0
  @enemies_destroyed = 0
  @game_music = Gosu::Song.new('sounds/Cephalopod.ogg')
  @game_music.play(true)
➤ @explosion_sound = Gosu::Sample.new('sounds/explosion.ogg')
➤ @shooting_sound = Gosu::Sample.new('sounds/shoot.ogg')
end
```

Explosions are created in the update_game() method, and you play the appropriate sound whenever you create a new one. Only the part of the update_game() method where you test for collisions between bullets and enemies is shown, with the new line highlighted:

SectorFive/SectorFive_4/sector_five_scenes.rb
```
@enemies.dup.each do |enemy|
  @bullets.dup.each do |bullet|
    distance = Gosu.distance(enemy.x, enemy.y, bullet.x, bullet.y)
```

```
      if distance < enemy.radius + bullet.radius
        @enemies.delete enemy
        @bullets.delete bullet
        @explosions.push Explosion.new(self, enemy.x, enemy.y)
        @enemies_destroyed += 1
➤       @explosion_sound.play
      end
    end
end
```

The shooting sound is a little loud and tends to get played quite a lot. You can tone it down by providing an optional volume argument to its play() method. Then you can still hear the background music:

SectorFive/SectorFive_4/sector_five_scenes.rb
```
def button_down_game(id)
  if id == Gosu::KbSpace
    @bullets.push Bullet.new(self,  @player.x, @player.y, @player.angle)
➤   @shooting_sound.play(0.3)
  end
end
```

Run the game and play it through. Make sure you die, fly off the top, and make it through at least one time each. Congratulations! You've finished the tutorial, and you've made a game, complete with tons of sprites, three scenes, and sounds. You might feel ready to make a completely new game, or you might first want to try making some changes to this one.

Make It Your Own

Now that the game is finished, you can take it anywhere you want. Here are some ideas to get you started. Feel free to do some or all of these, or to start from scratch with your own ideas.

Add another sound effect.
> Add a sound effect for when enemies reach the bottom of the screen. Find a sound distinct from the exploding enemy sound to alert the player that one got away.

Write the score on the screen.
> Use an instance of Gosu::Font to write the number of enemies destroyed on the screen during the game scene. You'll need to decide how big to make it, what color, and where.

Make two waves of enemies.
> Create a fourth scene that represents another wave of enemies, perhaps with different characteristics. If you made enemies that shoot at the

player in a previous chapter, or enemies that move differently, you could add them in now.

Add a boss.

A boss is an enemy that is much harder to kill, often with some new abilities to test the player. Make a boss scene with some appropriate music, and see whether your players are up to the task.

Share your game.

In its current form as a bunch of Ruby, picture, and sound files, your game will work only on a computer whose owner has set up Ruby as you did in Chapter 2, *Get Ready*, on page 5. In Chapter 10, *Package and Share Your Game*, on page 173, you will learn how to package your game for Mac or Windows, so others can use it just as they'd use any other application. If you'd like to share your game, you could skip ahead and do that now.

What's Next

You've completed a sprite-based game, in which the player controlled one sprite and others are managed by the program you wrote. Many games are of this type, and if you've worked through the tutorial to this point, you're ready to make your own sprite-based game. In the next chapter, you'll learn how to make a puzzle game, where the player moves pieces on a board by clicking and dragging them. Gosu still provides the framework, but you'll use it somewhat differently, focusing on user actions rather than on the update() method.

CHAPTER 7

Creating a Puzzle Game

In this chapter, you'll learn to make a completely different kind of game from Sector Five. Your next game, Twelve, is a puzzle game, and is played on a grid of squares.

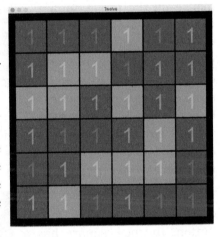

Players slide colored squares around a board, trying to combine as many like-colored squares as they can. In this game most of the action happens when the player clicks and drags from one square to another. The objects in Twelve are the squares themselves, which stay in place. As successful moves occur, squares change their color and number. To figure out what happens when such a move occurs, you'll focus on the rules of the game and learn how to translate those rules into code using a *flowchart*. In this chapter you'll learn to:

- Draw a layered image on the screen with colored squares and numbers.

- Handle mouse drags using Gosu's button_down() and button_up() methods.

- Create a flowchart to help figure out the result of a move.

- Translate the logic from the flowchart into code.

Puzzles are a fascinating class of games. Every few years, a puzzle game appears on the scene, and you see it everywhere. In 2014, the game *Threes* and its clones were on everyone's phones. A good puzzle game is simple to understand but difficult to master. Games of this sort are relatively easy to create and often have simple graphics, but making a great one is challenging.

When yours goes viral, I hope you'll take a moment to write me about it (from your beachside mansion).

When you start Twelve, the board looks something like the image at the start of the chapter on page 101, with twelve squares of each color randomly placed in a six-by-six grid. Because the colored squares are placed randomly, each game is a little different.

Players make moves by clicking on one square and dragging in a straight line onto a target square of the same color. When they release the mouse on the target square, the move is resolved. At the start of the game, the only possible moves are onto adjacent squares. As empty squares open up, moves can be made across them. If there

 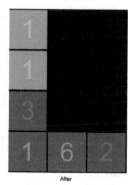

Before   After

are any empty squares on the other side of the target square, a move can continue into those. A region of the board is shown in the image, both before and after the player makes a move.

When the player completes the drag and releases the mouse button, the new square has a number in it that is the sum of the numbers that were in the two joined squares. The name of the game, Twelve, comes from the fact that the highest number you can get in a square is twelve. If you get three twelves, you've won the game.

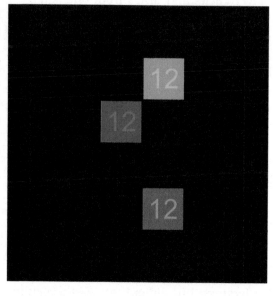

Getting three twelves requires some strategic thinking and maybe a little luck, because each starting board is different.

Great on a Tablet!

If you are working on a tablet or a touchscreen laptop running Windows, Twelve is even more fun. You can touch and drag squares with your finger, without using a keyboard or mouse.

You build Twelve in stages. First, you draw the board, at the same time setting up much of the structure of the game. Then you focus on the user interaction and game logic. Some of the finishing touches are left up to you, as you learned how to add sounds and create a starting scene in Chapter 6, *Adding Scenes and Sounds*, on page 79.

Drawing the Board

The game code is organized into three classes. The Twelve class is a subclass of Gosu::Window and has the Gosu run loop methods: initialize(), update(), and draw(). It also has the user-interaction methods button_down() and button_up(). Roughly speaking, the Twelve class is responsible for creating and maintaining the window on the screen and handling user input.

You create a separate class, Game, to handle the game logic. There is only one instance of the Game class at a time, and it has methods that take user input in the form of mouse down and mouse up locations, figures out whether those represent legal moves in the game, and then resolves those moves.

A third class, Square, contains the state of a single square and also draws that square. Each square has a color and a number, or is empty. Individual squares don't change position on the window. When a move is made, such as the move shown in the previous image, the numbers and colors of several squares are changed. Then the board is redrawn based on this new information the next time the draw() method of the Twelve class is executed.

Start by creating a folder called Twelve. In that folder, save three files called twelve.rb, game.rb, and square.rb to hold your three classes. First, write the Square class.

Making Squares

The main playing board of Twelve, as you can see in the original diagram on page 101, is a six-by-six grid of squares. Make each square 100 pixels on a side, and leave a 20-pixel border around the whole board, so your whole window will be 640 by 640 pixels. Squares will be identified by their row and column in the grid, each numbered from zero to five.

In square.rb, write the Square class and give it initialize() and draw() methods. That will be enough so that you can draw your board. The initialize() method takes row, column, and color values as arguments, as well as a reference to the window.

When you create the squares, each one has a @number value of 1. Use the symbols :red, :green, and :blue as values for the @color variable.

Because each square needs a reference to the same window, use a class variable, @@window, to hold that reference. You'll also use class variables @@font to draw the text and @@colors to hold a hash that associates the symbols :red, :green, and :blue with three instances of the Gosu::Color class. You'll set those class variables when you create the first instance of Square:

Twelve/Twelve_1/square.rb

```
require 'gosu'
class Square

  attr_reader :row, :column, :number, :color

  def initialize(window, column, row, color)
    @@colors ||= {red: Gosu::Color.argb(0xaaff0000),
                  green: Gosu::Color.argb(0xaa00ff00),
                  blue: Gosu::Color.argb(0xaa0000ff)}
    @@font ||= Gosu::Font.new(72)
    @@window ||= window
    @row = row
    @column = column
    @color = color
    @number = 1
  end
```

The Gosu::Color class has a method named argb() that takes as its argument an eight-digit hexadecimal number. Hexadecimal numbers in Ruby are written as 0x followed by the eight digits. The first two digits are the *alpha* or opacity of the color. The remaining digits are two for the amount of red, two for the amount of green, and two for the amount of blue, as shown in the following image.

These numbers can represent any color the screen can show, with any amount of transparency. Your three square colors are partially transparent, which will let the numbers show through from underneath.

Hexadecimal Numbers

Hexadecimal numbers use the numerals 0 through 9, along with the letters A through F, to represent decimal numbers between 0 and 255 using only two characters. The letter A equals ten, the letter B eleven, and so on, up to F, which equals fifteen. To find the decimal equivalent of a hexadecimal number, multiply the first digit by sixteen and add the second digit. So the hexadecimal C9 corresponds to (12 × 16) + 9 = 201. Hexadecimal numbers are often used to denote colors in computer code.

Drawing a Square

During the play of the game, some squares have numbers and colors, while other squares are empty. When a square becomes empty, you don't delete it from the array; instead, you set its @number variable to 0. An empty square might not remain empty, so your array will always have all thirty-six squares. When you draw a square, first check the value of @number. If @number isn't zero, you draw the square.

To draw a square, you need to figure out where on the window to put it, based on its @row and @column variables. Each square has a region 100 pixels on a side to occupy, and you'll leave a small, two-pixel black border around the edge of each square. This makes the colored part of the square 96 pixels on a side. You'll use the draw_quad() method to make the colored square, so you'll find the x and y values for all four corners, starting with the top-left corner. The other corners' positions are calculated from that one, as shown in the following image.

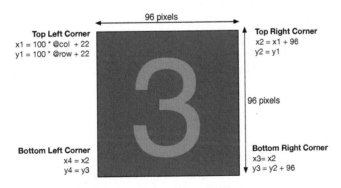

To draw the number exactly at the center of the square, calculate where you should place the left edge of the number. You can find the width of any text using the text_width() method of the Gosu::Font class. By subtracting half the width of the text from the x position of the center of the square, you can get the x position of the left edge of the text. Finding the y position of the text is simpler, since the text is all the same height, 72 pixels.

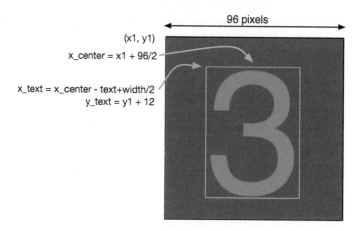

In the draw() method of the Square class, you draw the squares over the numbers by giving the squares a larger z value than the numbers:

```
Twelve/Twelve_1/square.rb
def draw
  if @number != 0
    x1 = 22 + @column * 100
    y1 = 22 + @row * 100
    x2 = x1 + 96
    y2 = y1
    x3 = x2
    y3 = y2 + 96
    x4 = x1
    y4 = y3
    c = @@colors[@color]
    @@window.draw_quad(x1, y1, c, x2, y2, c, x3, y3, c, x4, y4, c, 2)
    x_center = x1 + 48
    x_text = x_center - @@font.text_width("#{@number}") / 2
    y_text = y1 + 12
    @@font.draw("#{@number}", x_text, y_text, 1)
  end
end
```

Gosu doesn't really draw three-dimensional pictures, but it does let you choose which things are drawn on top by giving them greater z values. Because of this, you can think of the positive z direction as being up out of the screen. When you draw the colored, semitransparent square over the white number, you get numbers that contrast nicely with the colors of their squares.

Testing Some Squares

Before you move on to drawing the whole board, test your Square class to make sure things are working the way you want. When you're writing your own game, this sort of testing can be very helpful.

The simple test class creates two squares and then draws them. This class isn't part of your finished game, but leave it in the same folder as your game in case you want to use it again. Name the class SquareTest and put it in a file called square_test.rb:

Twelve/Twelve_1/square_test.rb

```ruby
require 'gosu'
require_relative 'square'

class SquareTest < Gosu::Window

  def initialize
    super(640, 640)
    self.caption = "Testing Squares"
    @square1 = Square.new(self, 0, 2, :blue)
    @square2 = Square.new(self, 1, 1, :red)
  end

  def draw
    @square1.draw
    @square2.draw
  end
end

window = SquareTest.new
window.show
```

When you run this small program, it draws two squares. The following image shows a region of the board containing these squares.

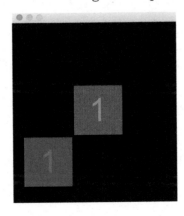

By changing the column and row values, you can draw the squares in different positions. Now that you can create and draw individual squares, you're ready to set up and draw the whole board.

A Grid of Squares

This game has thirty-six squares, in six columns and six rows. You create them in the initialize() method of the Game class and put them in an array called @squares. Once they are created, you draw them by iterating through the array and calling each square's draw() method.

When you create the squares, you can't just give each one a random color, since you want exactly twelve of each color. You handle this by creating an array, called color_list, with twelve elements each of :red, :green, and :blue. Then you randomize that array with the shuffle!() method of the Array class so that the colors are in random positions in the array, and there are still twelve of each. Then you create the squares in six rows and six columns, each numbered zero to five. Calculate a value, index = row * 6 + column, that is different for each square and use that element of the array to assign the color:

Twelve/Twelve_1/game.rb
```
require_relative 'square'

class Game
  def initialize(window)
    @window = window
    @squares = []
    color_list = []
    [:red, :green, :blue].each do |color|
      12.times do
        color_list.push color
      end
    end
    color_list.shuffle!
    (0..5).each do |row|
      (0..5).each do |column|
        index = row * 6 + column
        @squares.push Square.new(@window, column, row, color_list[index])
      end
    end
    @font = Gosu::Font.new(36)
  end
end
```

Now the @squares array has thirty-six squares, with twelve of each color. Put these squares into the array in order. Any time you have the row and column of a square, you can calculate its array index with the same calculation, index = row * 6 + column, that you used to assign its color.

Now give the Game class a draw() method to show the squares in the window. The hard part of drawing the board is already done, since each square can draw itself. You just iterate through the array of squares and draw each one:

Twelve/Twelve_1/game.rb
```
def draw
  @squares.each do |square|
    square.draw
  end
end
```

We'll come back to the Game class later, when it's time to handle the player's interaction with the squares. Now let's set up the Twelve class so that it draws the board.

In twelve.rb, put the Twelve class, and then use it to create your window. In the initialize() method, create a single instance of Game. In draw(), you can just call the draw() method of @game:

Twelve/Twelve_1/twelve.rb
```
require 'gosu'
require_relative 'game'

class Twelve < Gosu::Window

  def initialize
    super(640,640)
    self.caption = 'Twelve'
    @game = Game.new(self)
  end
  def draw
    @game.draw
  end


end

window = Twelve.new
window.show
```

When you run the game now, you see the game window with thirty-six squares. Remember to make sure you run twelve.rb, and not game.rb or square.rb. The board is ready. It's time to let the player make some moves.

Dragging a Square

Dragging from one square to another is at the heart of Twelve. A potential move is defined by which square the user mouses down on, along with the square where the user releases the mouse. You figure out whether the move from the first square to the second is valid. If it is, you execute the move, changing the numbers and colors of the appropriate squares. If it's not, you don't do anything at all, and the player can try again.

Before you start working with mouse clicks, you might notice that the mouse cursor does not appear when the mouse is in the window. For an arcade-style game this might be appropriate, but while playing Twelve, the user needs to see the mouse cursor. To make this change, add the following method to the Twelve class:

Twelve/Twelve_1/twelve.rb
```
def needs_cursor?
  true
end
```

If you're going to use this game only on a touchscreen laptop or tablet, you could leave this method out.

Mouse Down

When you mouse down in the window, you pass the location of the mouse click to a method of the Game class called handle_mouse_down():

Twelve/Twelve_1/twelve.rb
```
def button_down(id)
  if id == Gosu::MsLeft
    @game.handle_mouse_down(mouse_x, mouse_y)
  end
end
```

In the handle_mouse_down() method, you use a little math to figure out which square the player clicked on. This is the reverse of the math you did to draw a square at a particular row and column. If, for instance, a mouse click has an x value of 350, it is in column 3, which is actually the fourth column from the left.

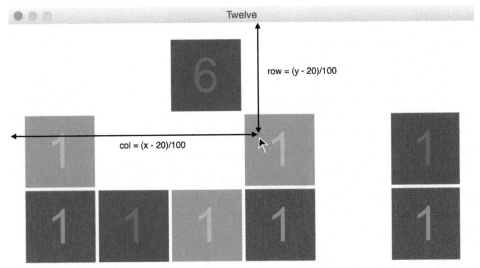

You do a similar calculation to find the row. Once you've figured out the row and column of the square, you get a reference to that square using a utility method, get_square(col,row), that you haven't yet written. The reference is saved in an instance variable, @start_square:

Twelve/Twelve_1/game.rb
```
def handle_mouse_down(x,y)
  row = (y.to_i - 20)/100
  column = (x.to_i - 20)/100
  @start_square = get_square(column, row)
end
```

The get_square() method first checks to make sure you haven't clicked outside the board. If you have, there is no square there, so no square should be returned. Assuming the click is inside the board, the appropriate square is returned. Note that the calculation of the index is the same as the one in the initialize() method:

Twelve/Twelve_1/game.rb
```
def get_square(column, row)
  if column < 0 or column > 5 or row < 0 or row > 5
    return nil
  else
    return @squares[row * 6 + column]
  end
end
```

Now that you've got the starting square safely stored, the next step is to figure out what happens when the player releases the mouse button.

Mouse Up

A move in Twelve starts when the player clicks on a square. In the previous section, you figured out which square was clicked on, and you saved a reference to that square in @start_square. The move ends when the player releases the mouse. At this point, if the move is valid, the contents of two squares will be combined and put into the square where the mouse up occurred. To figure out whether the move is valid, you first need to figure out which square the player's mouse cursor was in when the mouse button was released.

Just as Gosu::Window provides a button_down() method, it also provides a button_up() method, which fires when a key or mouse button is released. The button_up() method will look much like the button_down() method:

Twelve/Twelve_1/twelve.rb

```
def button_up(id)
  if id == Gosu::MsLeft
    @game.handle_mouse_up(mouse_x, mouse_y)
  end
end
```

The handle_mouse_up(x,y) method of the Game class does the same calculation that the handle_mouse_down(x,y) method does to find the row and column where the mouse up happened. Then the get_square() method is used to get a reference to that square, which is saved in @end_square. Check to make sure that the player actually dragged from one square to another, rather than into or from an area of the window with no squares. If both @start_square and @end_square refer to squares, meaning that neither is nil, you call the move() method and pass it both squares:

Twelve/Twelve_1/game.rb

```
def handle_mouse_up(x, y)
  row = (y.to_i - 20) / 100
  column = (x.to_i - 20) / 100
  @end_square = get_square(column, row)
  if @start_square and @end_square
    move(@start_square, @end_square)
  end
  @start_square = nil
end
```

In the move() method, you now have to figure out whether a move from @start_square to @end_square is valid. To do this, take a closer look at the rules and how you can express them in code.

Turn Rules into Code

The rules of the game seem simple enough. A drag is valid if it's within a row or a column, and if the two squares are the same color, and if there are no other squares between them. The drag can end on the second square, or it can continue onto empty squares beyond the second square. In this section you write the method, move(square1, square2), that makes these rules part of the game.

Make a Flowchart

To help you get from the rules to code, create a flowchart. A flowchart is a diagram that represents a set of rules in an organized way. Just making a flowchart like this can help you clarify what you really mean when you state the rules of a game. In a flowchart, conditionals are represented with diamonds, and calculations are represented by rectangles. Each conditional has two arrows leading out of it—one for YES and one for NO—while a rectangle has only one path out. The rules of Twelve that determine whether a particular move from @start_square to @end_square is valid are represented by the flowchart on page 114.

To determine whether the move is valid, the strategy followed by this flowchart is to go through all the things that would make a move *invalid* and test for those, one at a time. Any move that isn't invalid for any of these reasons must be valid.

Make Code from the Flowchart

To turn this flowchart into code, you'll first write a few supporting methods. In particular, the calculations required by the rectangles in the green box towards the top of the flowchart are complicated enough to make into their own methods.

One method, squares_between_in_row(square1, square2), takes two squares and returns an array of all the squares between those squares in a row. In the drag shown by the following image, the method returns an array of five squares.

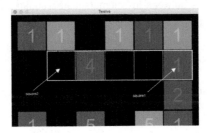

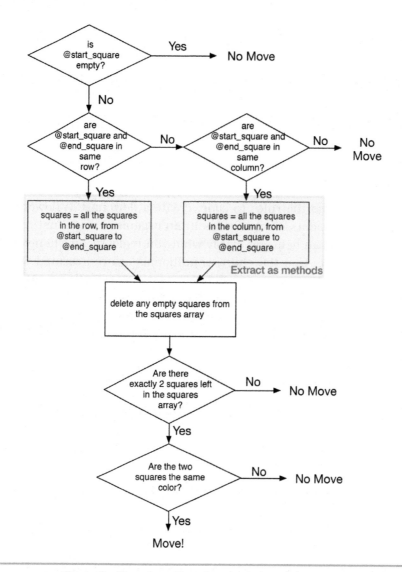

Figure 2—Flowchart Showing the Rules of the Game

A second method, squares_between_in_column(square1, square2), does the same thing for squares in a column:

Twelve/Twelve_1/game.rb
```ruby
def squares_between_in_row(square1, square2)
  the_squares = []
  if square1.column < square2.column
    column_start, column_end = square1.column, square2.column
  else
```

```
      column_start, column_end = square2.column, square1.column
    end
    (column_start .. column_end).each do |column|
      the_squares.push get_square(column, square1.row)
    end
    return the_squares
end

def squares_between_in_column(square1, square2)
  the_squares = []
  if square1.row < square2.row
    row_start, row_end = square1.row, square2.row
  else
    row_start, row_end = square2.row, square1.row
  end
  (row_start .. row_end).each do |row|
    the_squares.push get_square(square1.column, row)
  end
  return the_squares
end
```

Now you can write your move(square1, square2) method. Each of the diamonds in the flowchart represents a conditional statement. If one of the branches of the conditional leads to a "No Move" result, you'll simply return from your method. This causes nothing to happen, which is what you want:

Twelve/Twelve_1/game.rb
```
def move(square1, square2)
  return if square1.number == 0
  if square1.row == square2.row
    squares = squares_between_in_row(square1, square2)
  elsif square1.column == square2.column
    squares = squares_between_in_column(square1, square2)
  else
    return
  end
  squares.reject!{|square| square.number == 0}
  return if squares.count != 2
  return if squares[0].color != squares[1].color
  #valid move
end
```

If none of the four return statements is triggered, you have a valid move. You clear the two squares that were not empty and fill the square on which your move ended. The square you ended on might be one of the ones that had a value, or it might not. The strategy works either way.

To change the state of the squares, let's make some new methods in the Square class. One will clear a square, setting @number to zero. Another takes a number

and a color as arguments, and sets the square's @number and @color variables
to those values:

Twelve/Twelve_1/square.rb
```
def clear
  @number = 0
end

def set(color, number)
  @color = color
  @number = number
end
```

Then, at the end of the move(square1, square2) method of Game, you can clear the
two squares left in the squares array and set the color and number of square2,
which is where the move ended:

Twelve/Twelve_1/game.rb
```
color = squares[0].color
number = squares[0].number + squares[1].number
squares[0].clear
squares[1].clear
square2.set(color, number)
```

Now the game works. Play a few rounds and see whether you can get to three
twelves. One final annoyance is that you need to restart the game to play
again. Let's make it so we can play again more easily.

Play Again?

We let people play again by pressing Ctrl-R. We could more easily make it
just R, but then players might restart accidentally when they've almost won
a game. Because the button_down() method responds to each key press, rather
than to combinations of keys, let's check to see whether the R key is pressed
and then use the button_down?() method to see whether the Ctrl key is also being
pressed at that moment. To restart the game, all you need to do is call the
initialize() method of the Game class and replace @game with a new Game instance.
Add this to the button_down() method of the Twelve class:

Twelve/Twelve_1/twelve.rb
```
if id == Gosu::KbR && button_down?(Gosu::KbLeftControl)
  @game = Game.new(self)
end
```

That's a nice benefit you get from separating out the Game class. Since the
@game object represents a single game, you can replace it any time with a new
game. Now you can play over and over.

Add Visual Feedback

When you play Twelve now, all the action happens when the mouse button is released. When you click on a square and slide the mouse around, nothing appears to happen. In this section, you'll add highlights to the squares to give users some visual feedback about the move they are making.

First, as the player clicks on a square to begin a move, add a white square highlight to the starting square, as shown in the following image.

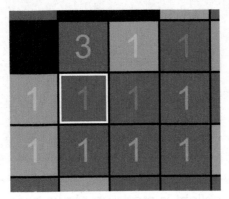

This square remains highlighted until the player releases the mouse, reminding the player which square is making the move.

As the player moves the mouse around to different squares, the square that the mouse cursor is in is also highlighted. If the move is a legal one, the highlight is green; if not, it is red.

Highlighted Illegal Move   Highlighted Legal Move

Each of these highlights is actually four rectangles, each four pixels in one dimension and ninety-six in the other. Two of these rectangles, on the top and bottom of the square, are oriented horizontally, while the other two are oriented vertically. These rectangles are shown outlined in red and green in the following image.

The highlight is made up of two horizontal rectangles, and two vertical rectangles.

The highlight rectangles overlap at the corners, but since all four are one color, they appear as the outline of a single square.

To make these highlights, you first make a new method in the Square class called highlight(state). The state argument is either :start, :legal, or :illegal, and it determines which color you draw the highlight rectangles. Two more methods, draw_horizontal_highlight(x1, y1, c) and draw_vertical_highlight(x1, y1, c), create the actual rectangles. The arguments x1 and y1 are the position of the top-left corner of the highlight rectangle:

Twelve/Twelve_1/square.rb
```
def highlight(state)
  case state
  when :start
    c = Gosu::Color::WHITE
  when :illegal
    c = Gosu::Color::RED
  when :legal
    c = Gosu::Color::GREEN
  end
  x1 = 22 + @column * 100
  y1 = 22 + @row * 100
```

```
    draw_horizontal_highlight(x1, y1, c)
    draw_horizontal_highlight(x1, y1 + 92, c)
    draw_vertical_highlight(x1, y1, c)
    draw_vertical_highlight(x1 + 92, y1, c)
end

def draw_horizontal_highlight(x1, y1, c)
  x2 = x1 + 96
  y2 = y1
  x3 = x1 + 96
  y3 = y1 + 4
  x4 = x1
  y4 = y1 + 4
  @@window.draw_quad(x1, y1, c, x2, y2, c, x3, y3, c, x4, y4, c, 3)
end

def draw_vertical_highlight(x1,y1,c)
  x2 = x1 + 4
  y2 = y1
  x3 = x1 + 4
  y3 = y1 + 92
  x4 = x1
  y4 = y1 + 92
  @@window.draw_quad(x1, y1, c, x2, y2, c, x3, y3, c, x4, y4, c, 3)
end
```

In the Twelve class, you implement the update() method, which you haven't
needed until now. You want to know where the mouse cursor is all the time,
so you can highlight the current square. In the update() method, you send the
mouse position to a new method of the Game class called handle_mouse_move(x,
y). There is a nice symmetry to this, since you already have methods called
handle_mouse_down(x, y) and handle_mouse_up(x, y):

Twelve/Twelve_1/twelve.rb
```
def update
  @game.handle_mouse_move(mouse_x, mouse_y)
end
```

In the Game class, you implement the handle_mouse_move method. This method
figures out which square the mouse is on and sets the value of @current_square:

Twelve/Twelve_1/game.rb
```
def handle_mouse_move(x, y)
  row = (y.to_i - 20) / 100
  column = (x.to_i - 20) / 100
  @current_square = get_square(column, row)
end
```

You write a new method, move_is_legal?(square1, square2), to help figure out what
highlight to apply to @current_square. This method is very similar to the

move(square1, square2) method, but it simply returns true or false and does not
execute the move:

```
Twelve/Twelve_1/game.rb
def move_is_legal?(square1, square2)
  return false if square1.number == 0
  if square1.row == square2.row
    squares = squares_between_in_row(square1, square2)
  elsif square1.column == square2.column
    squares = squares_between_in_column(square1, square2)
  else
    return false
  end
  squares.reject!{|square| square.number == 0}
  return false if squares.count != 2
  return false if squares[0].color != squares[1].color
  return true
end
```

Now you're ready to highlight the squares in the draw() method of the Game
class. You don't want any highlighting between moves, when the value of
@start_square is nil. You should also make sure @current_square is different from
@start_square before you give it a highlight:

```
Twelve/Twelve_1/game.rb
def draw
  @squares.each do |square|
    square.draw
  end
➤  return unless @start_square
➤  @start_square.highlight(:start)
➤  return unless @current_square && @current_square != @start_square
➤  if move_is_legal?(@start_square, @current_square)
➤    @current_square.highlight(:legal)
➤  else
➤    @current_square.highlight(:illegal)
➤  end
end
```

Now when you play, you get some more feedback, and the game is more fun.

Up until now, it has been up to the user to determine when there are no more
moves to make. You already have a method, move_is_legal(square1, square2), that
can tell you whether a single move is legal. In the next section, you'll use that
same method to test *every possible move* to find out whether there are *any*
legal moves left.

Check All the Moves

The game is over when there are no more moves for the player to make. Sometimes this is hard for players to figure out, and it's a nice touch to do it for them. Our strategy is to check every possible move until we find a legal one. If we don't find one, the game is over. You can create two new methods in the Game class to help you figure this out. The first one, legal_move_for?(start_square), will return true if start_square has any possible legal moves and false if it does not. First, it checks to see whether start_square is empty and returns false in this case. Then it checks the moves from start_square to every square on the board. If it finds a legal move, it returns true. If it does not, it returns false:

Twelve/Twelve_1/game.rb
```ruby
def legal_move_for?(start_square)
  return false if start_square.number == 0
  @squares.each do |end_square|
    if move_is_legal?(start_square, end_square)
      return true
    end
  end
  return false
end
```

The game_over?() checks each square. If it finds one with a legal move it returns false, because in this case the game is not over. If no square has a legal move, it returns true:

Twelve/Twelve_1/game.rb
```ruby
def game_over?
  @squares.each do |square|
    return false if legal_move_for?(square)
  end
  return true
end
```

When the game ends, you alert the player by drawing a translucent square over the whole board and writing "Game Over" over that. You also tell the player how to play again, and you stop highlighting the squares:

Twelve/Twelve_1/game.rb
```ruby
def draw
  @squares.each do |square|
    square.draw
  end
➤ if game_over?
➤   c = Gosu::Color.argb(0x33000000)
➤   @window.draw_quad(0, 0, c, 640, 0, c, 640, 640, c, 0, 640, c, 4)
```

```
➤        @font.draw('Game Over', 230, 240, 5)
➤        @font.draw('CTRL-R to Play Again', 205, 320, 5, 0.6, 0.6)
➤        return
➤      end
      return unless @start_square
      @start_square.highlight(:start)
      return unless @current_square && @current_square != @start_square
      if move_is_legal?(@start_square, @current_square)
        @current_square.highlight(:legal)
      else
        @current_square.highlight(:illegal)
      end
    end
```

When the game ends, the player can still see the board, though it is visibly darker. Clicking and moving the mouse no longer has any visible effect, since you return from the draw() method before the part that draws highlights.

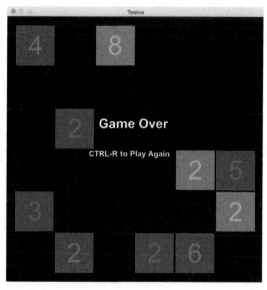

Twelve now helps players in two ways. Players can see whether the move they are currently making is legal, and Twelve lets them know when the game is over and there are no more moves to make. You should play a few times and think of ways you could make it even better.

Make It Your Own

Twelve is complete and fun now, but it's not really finished. Improving it could help you reinforce skills you learned earlier in this book, or could take you beyond what you've already done. Here are some ideas to get you started.

Add a start screen.

Break Twelve into two or more scenes—one that gives the user some instructions and one for the game. A really amazing start screen could even play an animation of a move.

Add some sounds.

Give Twelve some sound effects, maybe a happy "snick" for a successful move and something sadder for an unsuccessful one.

Add different visual cues.

The highlighted squares in *Add Visual Feedback*, on page 117, are just one possible way to give the player some feedback. Perhaps you can think of a way you like better. What if the actual result of legal moves was shown, perhaps in a somewhat different color?

Refactor some methods.

There is quite a bit of repeated code in Twelve, especially in some methods in the Game class. See if you can tighten up the code, perhaps by rewriting the move_is_legal?(square1, square2) method and the move(square1, square2) method so that one can be used by the other.

Let the player undo a move.

Make Ctrl-U or some other key press undo the last move. To do this, before you execute a move, you could create and save a copy of the whole @game object.

Make a better game.

Try changing the rules of Twelve to make it easier, harder, or just more fun. What happens if there are four colors? Diagonal moves?

What's Next

You've now tackled a sprite-based game and a puzzle game. Maybe you've come up with a great idea for a puzzle game of your own, and you want to get started. When you're ready, you can move on to the final game in this book. The last game will be a scrolling platformer, with a hero jumping between platforms and dodging boulders to escape a pit. You'll learn to use a physics engine to help you move objects more realistically and a camera object so your entire scene can be bigger than what your window shows.

CHAPTER 8

Making a Platformer Game with Physics

Our next game, Escape, is a *platformer* where the player controls a character that is trying escape a pit. The character, named Chip, runs and jumps between platforms while avoiding boulders that fall, spinning and bouncing, from above.

When boulders hit Chip, he doesn't fall down, but he may be knocked to a lower platform, or even all the way to the bottom of the pit. Chip's ascent out of the pit is timed; a shorter time is a better score.

Escape is a sprite game much like Sector Five. You'll make classes for each kind of sprite in the game: boulders, platforms, and Chip. The difference is that to make Chip jump and the boulders fall, bounce, and spin, you'll use a *physics engine*. As you add objects to the game, you'll describe their *properties* and then hand them over to the physics engine. The engine then takes over moving the objects. For instance, in the Boulder class, we provide some information: "Boulders are pretty heavy. They are affected by gravity and can rotate. They bounce off other objects like walls and platforms and have a certain amount of friction when they come in contact with other things." When we add boulders to our game we don't have to move them ourselves. Instead, the physics engine takes care of it. The boulders behave the way we said boulders should behave, and when we draw them we ask the physics engine where they are.

When it's time to make Chip run and jump by pressing keys on the keyboard, we don't move him directly. Instead we exert a *force* on him, and the physics engine does the calculations needed to figure out where he goes.

In this chapter, you'll:

- Use a physics engine to manage the motion of your objects.
- Add immovable objects to the game.
- Move objects in the game by applying forces.

We'll build Escape step by step, starting with the boulders that fall, tumble, and bounce according to the laws of physics. We'll add platforms, walls, and a floor, which don't move but which make the boulders bounce. Then we'll add Chip, who is our most complicated object. He is affected by gravity and can run and jump at our command. Finally, we'll add moving platforms that make the game more fun and challenging. In the next chapter, Chapter 9, *Making a Side-Scrolling Game*, on page 157, we'll improve Escape by making the pit deeper and adding a moving camera that follows the character.

Use a Physics Engine

The physics engine is called Chipmunk, and you can include it in your project using the Ruby gem of the same name. The Chipmunk gem provides several classes you can use to create objects. To understand how Chipmunk handles motion and interactions, take a look at some of these classes.

CP::Space

The game will have a single instance of the CP::Space class. This space is the object that holds all the objects that the physics engine manages. When you create a new object, such as a boulder or a platform, you add it to the space. The main method of the space is step(), which moves the game move forward in time. You call the step() method of the space in the game's update() method. The space also has some properties that affect all the objects you add to the space: gravity and damping.

CP::Body

Each object you add to the game has a body. The body object holds information about the position, velocity, mass, and rotational inertia of the object. For each object, you create the body and then add the body to the space.

CP::Shape

Each object also needs a shape. The shape of an object determines how it interacts with all the other objects. The shapes of all the objects in the game will be *polygons*. In addition to the actual boundaries of the object, the shape keeps track of information about how the object will interact with other objects. *Friction* and *elasticity* are two properties of the shape that help determine what happens when two objects come into contact.

CP::Vec2

Many of the quantities that Chipmunk uses are *vectors*, with a horizontal part and a vertical part. This class allows us to create a single object with two components, x and y, to hold such a value.

The Laws of Physics

There are many laws of physics—laws about electricity and magnetism, laws about heat and temperature, and laws about the bending of light. The ones we're talking about in this chapter are Newton's three laws of motion. These laws are pretty famous, and you may have heard of them.

The first law states that an object in motion will remain in motion. Objects have inertia, and the more *mass* they have, the harder it is to stop them or to get them moving.

Newton's second law states that if you want to get an object moving or change the motion of an object, you have to exert a *force* on it. An equation, $F = ma$, governs this relationship. The F stands for force, the m for mass, and the a for acceleration. Understanding this equation will help you figure out how large to make the masses and forces in the game.

The third law concerns the interactions between objects. When one object pushes on another, it is pushed back in return with the same force. When a boulder knocks Chip off a platform, the boulder will be pushed in the other direction.

Chipmunk works by applying these laws to all the objects that have been added to the physics space. By giving objects different masses and applying forces to the objects, you can control what happens in the game.

Find the folder called Escape_Starter in the book files you downloaded earlier. Make a copy of that folder named Escape and take a look through its contents.

There are many images you need to build Escape, along with a Ruby file for the game, escape.rb. The game is still based on the Gosu::Window class, and so your initial setup is not very different from the games you've made already. The only change so far is that you need the Chipmunk gem in addition to Gosu.

Set up the physics engine in the initialize() method of the Escape class by adding the space object that will hold and update all of your physics objects. You can also set a background image here for the game. Because you will be drawing this image more than once to fill the space, set its tileabe option to true. The background image won't interact with any of the objects, so you don't add it to the physics space.

Escape/Escape_1/escape.rb
```
require 'gosu'
require 'chipmunk'
class Escape < Gosu::Window
  attr_reader :space
  def initialize
    super(800,800)
    self.caption = 'Escape'
    @game_over = false
    @space = CP::Space.new
    @background = Gosu::Image.new('images/background.png', tileable: true)
  end
end

window = Escape.new
window.show
```

There are two properties of the space that you configure, damping and gravity. Damping is a number that determines how much things will slow down on their own. A damping of 1.0 means objects in the space would never slow down. A damping of 0.9 means that each object in the space will lose 10 percent of its velocity each second, if there are no other forces on it. Use a constant for this value to make it easy to adjust. You did something like this on your own with the spaceship in *Move the Ship*, on page 44.

Gravity exerts a force on everything in the space. Chipmunk lets us set a value for gravity that points in any direction; it is represented by a Cp::Vec2 object that has a horizontal, or x, part and a vertical, or y, part. You want your gravity to point straight down, with only a vertical part, but you may want to adjust its strength. To represent gravity, create a single constant, GRAVITY, and set its value to 400.0. In the initialize() method of the Escape class, set the value of @space.gravity to a vector that you create using the GRAVITY constant.

Escape/Escape_1/escape.rb

```
class Escape < Gosu::Window
➤  DAMPING = 0.90
➤  GRAVITY = 400.0
   attr_reader :space
   def initialize
     super(800,800)
     self.caption = 'Escape'
     @game_over = false
     @space = CP::Space.new
     @background = Gosu::Image.new('images/background.png', tileable: true)
➤    @space.damping = DAMPING
➤    @space.gravity = CP::Vec2.new(0.0, GRAVITY)
   end
```

Now any objects you add to your space will be pulled toward the bottom of the window. As soon as you add boulders to the space, they will start to fall.

In the update() method of the game, you tell the physics engine to *step* forward in time. While the update() method runs about sixty times per second, you want your physics to step forward in even smaller increments. When objects are moving quickly, they might overlap by a large amount in one sixtieth of a second. By having the physics engine update ten times every update(), or six hundred times per second, your physics will be more realistic. If your computer can't handle this rate, you can back off a bit, but Chipmunk has been written to be very quick and efficient. Here is the update() method of the game:

Escape/Escape_1/escape.rb

```
def update
  unless @game_over
    10.times do
      @space.step(1.0/600)
    end
  end
end
```

Your game is set up, with a space ready for you to add objects. Now you can add some boulders that tumble down from above.

Make Boulders Fall

In Chapter 4, *Creating a Sprite-Based Game*, on page 39, you learned to make classes for each type of sprite in the game. You made classes for the player ship, for the enemies, and for bullets and explosions. When you create sprites that will be moved by the physics engine, you still make classes, but those classes do things a little differently.

Bodies, Shapes, and Images

When you add a boulder to the game, you describe it by giving it some physical properties and a shape, and then you add it to the space. You also give it an image that matches its shape. If the image you choose and the shape you define match up reasonably well, the illusion of bouncing, spinning boulders is convincing. If they don't, the boulders look strange as they bounce off each other and off the platforms.

Make a new file, boulder.rb, to hold the Boulder class. In the initialize() method of the class, first create the body. Bodies are initialized with two arguments, *mass* and *rotational inertia*. Mass is a measure of resistance to changes in the velocity of the body, and rotational inertia is a measure of resistance to changes in rotation. You also set the position of the body and its maximum speed, called v_limit:

```
Escape/Escape_1/boulder.rb
class Boulder
  SPEED_LIMIT = 500
  attr_reader :body, :width, :height
  def initialize(window, x, y)
    @body = CP::Body.new(400, 4000)
    @body.p = CP::Vec2.new(x, y)
    @body.v_limit = SPEED_LIMIT
  end
end
```

The maximum speed, or v_limit, that you give each sprite in the game has a large effect on the gameplay. If you're looking to adjust the game to make gameplay easier or harder, changing the v_limit of some of your sprites is a good place to start.

Next, you create the shape. To create a shape that matches the image, take a very, very close look at the image on page 131. In this picture you can see the individual pixels. The gray and white checkerboard pattern is not part of the image, but rather how many image editors indicate transparent pixels. The red dots aren't part of the image, either; one marks the center, and the others are the vertices, or corners, of a *polygon* that will be the shape of the boulder object in the physics space.

You can find the position of each vertex, relative to the center, by counting pixels, remembering that the positive y direction is down. Then you put the ten vertices of the polygon, each a CP::Vec2 object, in an array called bounds. The vertices must be specified in a counterclockwise direction around the

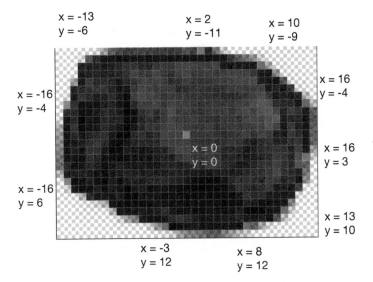

x = -13
y = -6

x = 2
y = -11

x = 10
y = -9

x = -16
y = -4

x = 16
y = -4

x = 0
y = 0

x = 16
y = 3

x = -16
y = 6

x = 13
y = 10

x = -3
y = 12

x = 8
y = 12

polygon, and the polygon must be *convex*, meaning that it doesn't have any indentations.[1] If you break any of these rules, you'll get an error like this one.

```
/Users/mark/Desktop/Escape/boulder.rb:24 in `initialize': The verts array
does not form a valid polygon! (ArgumentError)
```

Using the bounds array, you create the shape, which is attached to the body. You set two more properties of the shape—its *coefficient of friction*, named u, and its *elasticity*, named e. You also set @width and @height variables, which aren't used by the physics engine but which you'll use later to test whether Chip is standing on a boulder.

Then you finish by adding both the body and the shape to the space, and creating the @image variable. Add the following to the initialize() method of the Boulder class:

Escape/Escape_1/boulder.rb
```
class Boulder
➤   FRICTION = 0.7
➤   ELASTICITY = 0.95
    SPEED_LIMIT = 500
    attr_reader :body, :width, :height
    def initialize(window, x, y)
      @body = CP::Body.new(400, 4000)
      @body.p = CP::Vec2.new(x, y)
      @body.v_limit = SPEED_LIMIT
```

---

1.   http://en.wikipedia.org/wiki/Convex_and_concave_polygons

```
➤        bounds = [CP::Vec2.new(-13, -6),
➤                  CP::Vec2.new(-16, -4),
➤                  CP::Vec2.new(-16, 6),
➤                  CP::Vec2.new(-3, 12),
➤                  CP::Vec2.new(8, 12),
➤                  CP::Vec2.new(13, 10),
➤                  CP::Vec2.new(16, 3),
➤                  CP::Vec2.new(16, -4),
➤                  CP::Vec2.new(10, -9),
➤                  CP::Vec2.new(2, -11)]
➤        shape = CP::Shape::Poly.new(@body, bounds, CP::Vec2.new(0, 0))
➤        shape.u = FRICTION
➤        shape.e = ELASTICITY
➤        @width = 32
➤        @height = 32
➤        window.space.add_body(@body)
➤        window.space.add_shape(shape)
➤        @image = Gosu::Image.new('images/boulder.png')
    end
```

To draw a boulder, you get the position and angle from the @body object. Since Chipmunk measures angles in radians and Gosu measures angles in degrees, you need to convert the angle before you use it:

Escape/Escape_1/boulder.rb
```
def draw
  @image.draw_rot(@body.p.x, @body.p.y, 1, @body.angle * (180.0 / Math::PI))
end
```

The initialize() and draw() methods are the only ones you write for the Boulder class. There is no move() method, since the physics engine moves the boulders for us. The boulders are now ready to be shaken loose and fall into the pit.

Adding Boulders

You want your boulders to fall from above, at random times and in random directions, to create a sense of crazy chaos. To do this, create boulders just off the top of the screen, at a random horizontal position. Give each one a shove in a random direction. Start by adding the boulder.rb file in your project:

Escape/Escape_1/escape.rb
```
require 'gosu'
require 'chipmunk'
➤ require_relative 'boulder'
```

Then create an empty array to hold the boulders in the initialize() method of the Escape class:

Escape/Escape_1/escape.rb
```ruby
def initialize
  super(800,800)
  self.caption = 'Escape'
  @game_over = false
  @space = CP::Space.new
  @background = Gosu::Image.new('images/background.png', tileable: true)
  @space.damping = DAMPING
  @space.gravity = CP::Vec2.new(0.0, GRAVITY)
➤ @boulders = []
end
```

Add boulders at random times, about one frame in one hundred. This is similar to how you added enemies to Sector Five in Chapter 5, *Managing Lots of Sprites*, on page 57. Because you will likely want to adjust this frequency, you should first create a constant, called BOULDER_FREQUENCY:

Escape/Escape_1/escape.rb
```ruby
class Escape < Gosu::Window
  DAMPING = 0.90
  GRAVITY = 400.0
➤ BOULDER_FREQUENCY = 0.01
```

In the update() method of the Escape class, add the boulders to the game. Each is just off the top of the window, at a random horizontal position between one quarter and three quarters of the window width:

Escape/Escape_1/escape.rb
```ruby
def update
  unless @game_over
    10.times do
      @space.step(1.0/600)
    end
➤   if rand < BOULDER_FREQUENCY
➤     @boulders.push Boulder.new(self, 200 + rand(400), -20)
➤   end
  end
end
```

Give each boulder a push to get it started. Chipmunk gives you a method in the Cp::Body class, apply_impulse(), to apply an *instantaneous* force to an object. A force applied this way will get the object moving, but then lets it move on its own. When you kick a ball into the air, the kick gets it moving, but then gravity takes over. Your kick supplies an *impulse*. The apply_impulse() method takes two arguments, both of type CP::Vec2. The first argument is *how much* force to apply. The second is *where* to apply the force, relative to the center of the object, as shown in the following image:

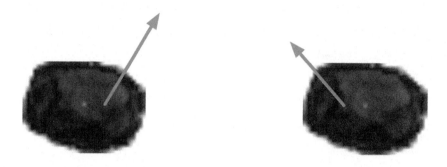

Each boulder gets a random push that makes it move and spin.

Applying the force away from the center makes the boulder spin. When you make both arguments random, the player doesn't know what will happen next and must keep a sharp eye out for falling boulders. Put the highlighted code at the end of the initialize() method of the Boulder class:

Escape/Escape_1/boulder.rb

```
def initialize(window, x, y)
  @body = CP::Body.new(400, 4000)
  @body.p = CP::Vec2.new(x, y)
  @body.v_limit = SPEED_LIMIT
  bounds = [CP::Vec2.new(-13, -6),
            CP::Vec2.new(-16, -4),
            CP::Vec2.new(-16, 6),
            CP::Vec2.new(-3, 12),
            CP::Vec2.new(8, 12),
            CP::Vec2.new(13, 10),
            CP::Vec2.new(16, 3),
            CP::Vec2.new(16, -4),
            CP::Vec2.new(10, -9),
            CP::Vec2.new(2, -11)]
  shape = CP::Shape::Poly.new(@body, bounds, CP::Vec2.new(0, 0))
  shape.u = FRICTION
  shape.e = ELASTICITY
  @width = 32
  @height = 32
  window.space.add_body(@body)
  window.space.add_shape(shape)
  @image = Gosu::Image.new('images/boulder.png')
➤ @body.apply_impulse(CP::Vec2.new(rand(100000) - 50000, 100000),
➤                     CP::Vec2.new(rand * 0.8 - 0.4, 0))
  end
```

To draw the background and boulders, add a draw() method to the Escape class. The background image doesn't fill the whole window, so draw it twice:

Escape/Escape_1/escape.rb
```ruby
def draw
  @background.draw(0,0,0)
  @background.draw(0,529,0)
  @boulders.each do |boulder|
    boulder.draw
  end
end
```

Run the game now, and boulders will fall from above at random intervals and in random directions:

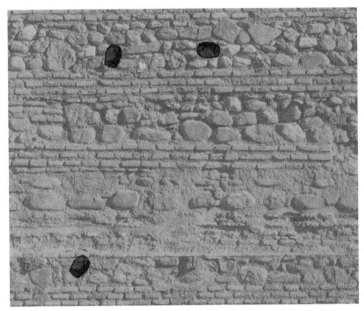

Gravity makes the boulders accelerate toward the ground, which means they will go faster and faster until they reach the speed limit you set for them. The force of gravity on a boulder will be the value you set for gravity, 400, multiplied by the mass of the boulder, which is also 400. This force of 160,000 is divided by the mass of the boulder to find its acceleration, which is 400. So each second the boulder will change its velocity by 400 in the downward direction. Two things act to slow down the boulders. First, the space has a damping that slows everything down a bit. Also, the speed of the boulders is capped at 500 pixels per second, so they don't fall too fast for Chip to avoid them.

You now have boulders that fall from above and down past the bottom of the window. The next objects to add are some platforms for the hero to climb and for the boulders to bounce off.

Make Stationary Walls and Platforms

Many of the objects in the game are *stationary*. When a boulder hits a platform, it will bounce and tumble, but the platform won't move at all. You also add walls to keep things from falling off the edges of the game, as well as a floor at the bottom. Chipmunk provides a way to add objects to the game that interact with all the other objects in the space but that do not move themselves.

Static Bodies

When you made your boulders, you started by giving them a *body* that had a mass and a rotational inertia. The platforms and walls don't have those properties; they simply don't move no matter what hits them. Chipmunk provides a special initializer for CP::Body that creates just such a *static* body, new_static(). It's possible to move an object with a static body by directly setting the values of its position, but the physics engine won't move it for you.

The platforms are all the same. Their image is 96 pixels wide and 16 pixels tall, so their shape will be a rectangle—a polygon with four vertices:

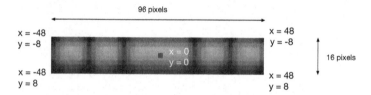

When you add static objects to the physics space, you add their shape but not their body. Since the object won't move anyway, the physics space has no use for the body object. Here is the code for the Platform class:

Escape/Escape_1/platform.rb
```ruby
class Platform
  FRICTION = 0.7
  ELASTICITY = 0.8
  attr_reader :body, :width, :height
  def initialize(window, x, y)
    space = window.space
    @width = 96
    @height = 16
    @body = CP::Body.new_static
    @body.p = CP::Vec2.new(x,y)
    bounds = [CP::Vec2.new(-48, -8),
              CP::Vec2.new(-48,  8),
              CP::Vec2.new(48,  8),
              CP::Vec2.new(48, -8)]
```

```
    shape = CP::Shape::Poly.new(@body, bounds, CP::Vec2.new(0, 0))
    shape.u = FRICTION
    shape.e = ELASTICITY
    space.add_shape(shape)
    @image = Gosu::Image.new('images/platform.png')
  end

  def draw
    @image.draw_rot(@body.p.x, @body.p.y, 1, 0)
  end
end
```

Add a few platforms near the bottom to see how the boulders interact with the platforms. First, you require the Platform class in escape.rb:

Escape/Escape_1/escape.rb
```
require 'gosu'
require 'chipmunk'
require_relative 'boulder'
➤ require_relative 'platform'
```

You'll be adding a bunch of platforms to your game, so add a new method, make_platforms(), that creates all the platforms and returns an array of platforms. For now, you add just four:

Escape/Escape_1/escape.rb
```
def make_platforms
  platforms = []
  platforms.push Platform.new(self,150,700)
  platforms.push Platform.new(self,320,650)
  platforms.push Platform.new(self,150,500)
  platforms.push Platform.new(self,470,550)
  return platforms
end
```

You call this method in the initialize() method of the Escape class, where you create a new instance variable, @platforms, to hold the array of platforms:

Escape/Escape_1/escape.rb
```
def initialize
  super(800,800)
  self.caption = 'Escape'
  @game_over = false
  @space = CP::Space.new
  @background = Gosu::Image.new('images/background.png', tileable: true)
  @space.damping = DAMPING
  @space.gravity = CP::Vec2.new(0.0, GRAVITY)
  @boulders = []
➤ @platforms = make_platforms
end
```

In the draw() method of the Escape class, draw the platforms:

Escape/Escape_1/escape.rb
```ruby
def draw
  @background.draw(0,0,0)
  @background.draw(0,529,0)
  @boulders.each do |boulder|
    boulder.draw
  end
  @platforms.each do |platform|
    platform.draw
  end
end
```

When you run the game now, the boulders fall and hit the platforms. The boulders bounce and spin. When they hit a corner, they spin even more. This is the physics engine at work—you'd have had a hard time making the boulders behave so convincingly without it. In fact, you'd have to write a physics engine!

Walls and a Floor

By adding walls and a floor, you keep your game objects in the window. All the boulders that fall stick around, and the player stops at the walls. By making the right wall a little shorter than the left, you allow Chip to run out of the window at the top right, ending the game. You put the walls and floor just off the screen, so you don't need to draw them at all. Give them static bodies and shapes, and the physics engine will take care of the rest.

You use one class, called Wall, for both the floor and the walls. To set the shapes, choose a rectangle that extends exactly to the edge of the screen. By making the position and size of the wall arguments of the initialize() method, you can create rectangular walls of any size:

Escape/Escape_1/wall.rb
```ruby
class Wall
  FRICTION = 0.7
  ELASTICITY = 0.2
  def initialize(window, x, y, width, height)
    space = window.space
    @x = x
    @y = y
    @width = width
    @height = height
    @body = CP::Body.new_static()
    @body.p = CP::Vec2.new(x,y)
    @bounds = [CP::Vec2.new(-width / 2, -height / 2),
               CP::Vec2.new(-width / 2, height / 2),
```

```
                CP::Vec2.new(width / 2, height / 2),
                CP::Vec2.new(width / 2, -height / 2)]
    @shape = CP::Shape::Poly.new(@body, @bounds, CP::Vec2.new(0, 0))
    @shape.u = FRICTION
    @shape.e = ELASTICITY
    space.add_shape(@shape)
  end
end
```

The initialize() method is the only method of the Wall class. Once you create the walls and add them to the space, the physics engine takes care of all their interactions.

In the escape.rb file, import the Wall class:

Escape/Escape_1/escape.rb
```
require 'gosu'
require 'chipmunk'
require_relative 'boulder'
require_relative 'platform'
➤ require_relative 'wall'
```

Now you can add two walls and a floor to the game. Each makes a rectangle that comes just to the edge of the window and prevents boulders from bouncing or falling out of view. The left wall is 800 pixels tall, blocking the whole left side. The right wall is only 660 pixels tall, so that Chip can escape when he reaches the top of the pit. Add the following just after the code that adds the platforms, in the initialize() method of the Escape class:

Escape/Escape_1/escape.rb
```
@floor = Wall.new(self, 400,810,800,20)
@left_wall = Wall.new(self, -10, 400, 20,800)
@right_wall = Wall.new(self, 810,470,20,660)
```

When you run your game now, the boulders bounce off the walls as well as the platforms. When the boulders hit the ground, they bounce a bit and come to rest. You've set the scene; now it's time for Chip to make his appearance.

Use Physics to Move a Character

The hero, Chip, is an object in the physics space as well. He can be knocked off course by boulders and will be stopped by walls, platforms, and the floor. Chip will also run and jump when you press the arrow keys and spacebar. You move him by exerting forces on him while the keys are pressed.

Create a new file to hold the Chip class, chip.rb. In initialize(), you first create Chip's physics properties, @body and @shape. Chip's mass will be 50, which is one-eighth the mass of a boulder.

When Chip runs, you want him to *look* like he is running. To achieve this, you use a sprite sheet for his image, much like the one you used to animate the explosions in *Make Animated Explosions*, on page 70. This sprite sheet has eight images and is shown in the following image.

Chip stands tall throughout the game. Boulders can push him back and even send him back to the ground, but they can't knock him down. To make sure Chip doesn't rotate, we set his rotational inertia to a seemingly strange thing, 100.0/0. Your math teacher probably told you that you aren't allowed to divide by zero, but Chipmunk is okay with it. When Chipmunk sees a value like this, it treats it like *infinity*. If Chip's rotational inertia is infinity, it means he won't rotate, no matter how much he is pushed.

Chip's shape, to keep things simple, is a rectangle. The height of the rectangle is the same as the height of the image, 64 pixels. The width of the rectangle is 20 pixels, which is an approximation of Chip's width. You can see a rectangle of this size superimposed on Chip in the following image.

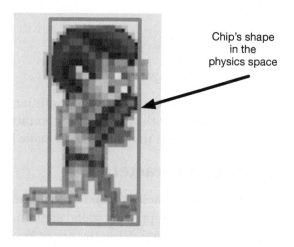

Chip's shape
in the
physics space

After you add Chip to the physics space, create a few more variables. The first, @action, keeps track of what Chip is doing so the appropriate images can be drawn. You'll draw Chip differently depending on whether he is running, jumping, or standing. Use the @image_index variable to show a sequence of images from the @images array when Chip is running. The @off_ground variable keeps track of whether Chip is on solid ground. If he's in the air, he can still control his motion *some*, but much less than when he is on firm ground.

Make four constants for the impulses you exert on Chip when he moves. RUN_IMPULSE and JUMP_IMPULSE are for when Chip is on the ground, and FLY_IMPULSE and (for lack of a better term) AIR_JUMP_IMPULSE are for when Chip's feet are off the ground. The jump impulses are much larger than the move impulses. This is due to the fact that you use the once-per-press button_down(key) method for jumping and the once-per-frame button_down?(key) method for moving left and right:

Escape/Escape_1/chip.rb
```
class Chip
  RUN_IMPULSE = 600
  FLY_IMPULSE = 60
  JUMP_IMPULSE = 36000
  AIR_JUMP_IMPULSE = 1200
  SPEED_LIMIT = 400
  FRICTION = 0.7
  ELASTICITY = 0.2
  attr_accessor :off_ground
  def initialize(window, x, y)
    @window = window
    space = window.space
    @images = Gosu::Image.load_tiles('images/chip.png', 40, 65)
    @body = CP::Body.new(50, 100 / 0.0)
    @body.p = CP::Vec2.new(x, y)
    @body.v_limit = SPEED_LIMIT
    bounds = [CP::Vec2.new(-10, -32),
              CP::Vec2.new(-10, 32),
              CP::Vec2.new(10, 32),
              CP::Vec2.new(10, -32)]
    shape = CP::Shape::Poly.new(@body, bounds, CP::Vec2.new(0, 0))
    shape.u = FRICTION
    shape.e = ELASTICITY
    space.add_body(@body)
    space.add_shape(shape)
    @action = :stand
    @image_index = 0
    @off_ground = true
  end
end
```

Require the file in escape.rb:

```
.pe/Escape_1/escape.rb
  equire 'gosu'
require 'chipmunk'
require_relative 'boulder'
require_relative 'platform'
require_relative 'wall'
➤ require_relative 'chip'
```

Then, at the end of the initialize() method of the Escape class, add Chip and place him near the bottom-left corner of the window:

```
Escape/Escape_1/escape.rb
def initialize
  super(800,800)
  self.caption = 'Escape'
  @game_over = false
  @space = CP::Space.new
  @background = Gosu::Image.new('images/background.png', tileable: true)
  @space.damping = DAMPING
  @space.gravity = CP::Vec2.new(0.0, GRAVITY)
  @boulders = []
  @platforms = make_platforms
  @floor = Wall.new(self, 400,810,800,20)
  @left_wall = Wall.new(self, -10, 400, 20,800)
  @right_wall = Wall.new(self, 810,470,20,660)
➤  @player = Chip.new(self,70,700)
end
```

Now that the hero is in the scene and has been added to the physics space, gravity will pull him down, and boulders can knock him around. But you can't see Chip until you draw him.

Draw the Character

The image you draw for Chip each frame will depend on what he is doing. You're using the @action variable to keep track of this. You'll change the value of @action in the update() method in the next section; for now, assume @action has one of the following values: :stand, :run_right, :run_left, :jump_right, or :jump_left. In the draw() method of the Chip class, check to see what the hero is doing and draw the appropriate image.

When Chip is running, draw a sequence of images. If you were to change the image every frame, or one-sixtieth of a second, Chip's feet would just be a blur. By adding 0.2 to the @image_index each frame, you draw the same image for five frames and then switch images. After the seventh image, you rotate back to the first using the modulo (%) operator. If Chip is jumping or standing, draw just the first image in the sprite sheet.

You may have noticed that in all the images in Chip's sprite sheet, he is facing to the right. The draw_rot() method provides a way to flip those images horizontally when you draw them, by setting an optional parameter called scale_x to -1. The draw() method of the Chip class looks like the following:

```
Escape/Escape_1/chip.rb
def draw
  case @action
  when :run_right
    @images[@image_index].draw_rot(@body.p.x, @body.p.y, 2, 0)
    @image_index = (@image_index + 0.2) % 7
  when :stand, :jump_right
    @images[0].draw_rot(@body.p.x, @body.p.y, 2, 0)
  when :run_left
    @images[@image_index].draw_rot(@body.p.x, @body.p.y, 2, 0, 0.5, 0.5, -1, 1)
    @image_index = (@image_index + 0.2) % 7
  when :jump_left
    @images[0].draw_rot(@body.p.x, @body.p.y, 2, 0, 0.5, 0.5, -1, 1)
  else
    @images[0].draw_rot(@body.p.x, @body.p.y, 2, 0)
  end
end
```

In the draw() method of the Escape class, draw Chip:

```
Escape/Escape_1/escape.rb
def draw
  @background.draw(0,0,0)
  @background.draw(0,529,0)
  @boulders.each do |boulder|
    boulder.draw
  end
  @platforms.each do |platform|
    platform.draw
  end
➤ @player.draw
end
```

When you run your game now, Chip appears just above the floor, and gravity pulls him down. If you wait a while, a boulder will knock Chip aside, one way or another. If you wait a long time, boulders will bury Chip. Let's get Chip moving so that he can escape the pit before he is buried.

Exert Forces on the Character

In Escape, you press the right or left arrow key to make Chip run and the spacebar to make him jump. He jumps and runs *if* his feet are touching something solid. If he is airborne, you can allow him to adjust his motion *a little*. He is a hero, after all. In update(), first check whether he is grounded and set his @off_ground instance variable.

@player.check_footing (@platforms + @boulders)

Create a new method in Chip, called touching?(footing). You're going to pass various objects as the footing parameter. Sometimes footing will be a boulder, but other times it will be a platform. In each case, you'll treat the object as a rectangle with a position given by x and y, a width, and a height. You'll also treat Chip's feet as a rectangle. Make the rectangle for Chip's feet extend a little beyond the rectangle that makes up his shape, as shown in the following image.

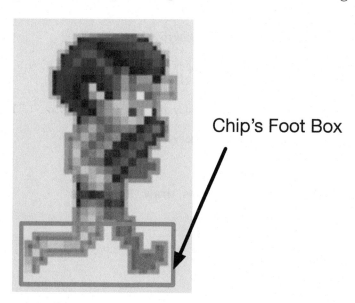

Chip's Foot Box

Do this just to make sure that if the physics engine detects a boulder or platform under Chip, your method also detects the object and allows him to jump. If you cut it too close, the physics engine might stop him from moving while your touching?() method did not detect any overlap. This would make your game break, since Chip couldn't move. Here is the touching?(footing) method that detects whether a given object is in contact with Chip's feet. It tests whether the rectangle of the footing object overlaps Chip's foot box:

Escape/Escape_1/chip.rb
```
def touching?(footing)
  x_diff = (@body.p.x - footing.body.p.x).abs
  y_diff = (@body.p.y + 30 - footing.body.p.y).abs
  x_diff < 12 + footing.width/2 and y_diff < 5 + footing.height / 2
end
```

Then give Chip another method, check_footing(things). This method will set a value for @off_ground. This method takes as an argument an array of objects to check, which includes all the boulders and platforms. It also checks to see whether Chip is touching the floor. If Chip's feet are touching any of these things, he can run and jump:

Escape/Escape_1/chip.rb
```
def check_footing(things)
  @off_ground = true
  things.each do |thing|
    @off_ground = false if touching?(thing)
  end
  if @body.p.y > 765
    @off_ground = false
  end
end
```

To make Chip run left and right, you don't just move him like you did the spaceship. Instead, you give him a push. You push him as long as the arrow keys are being pressed. In the update() method of Escape, add the following code:

Escape/Escape_1/escape.rb
```
if button_down?(Gosu::KbRight)
    @player.move_right
elsif button_down?(Gosu::KbLeft)
  @player.move_left
else
  @player.stand
end
```

We use the button_down() method to let Chip jump, checking for the spacebar. In this method, you also let the player quit the game by pressing the Q key:

Escape/Escape_1/escape.rb
```
def button_down(id)
  if id == Gosu::KbSpace
    @player.jump
  end
  if id == Gosu::KbQ
    close
  end
end
```

This gives you some methods to implement in the Chip class. In each of the methods move_right() and move_left(), you do two things. The first is that you set the variable @action, so that Chip is drawn correctly. The second is that we push Chip in the appropriate direction with the apply_impulse() method. You apply different impulses to Chip depending on whether his feet are touching the ground:

Escape/Escape_1/chip.rb
```
def move_right
  if @off_ground
    @action = :jump_right
    @body.apply_impulse(CP::Vec2.new(FLY_IMPULSE, 0), CP::Vec2.new(0, 0))
  else
    @action = :run_right
    @body.apply_impulse(CP::Vec2.new(RUN_IMPULSE,0 ), CP::Vec2.new(0, 0))
  end
end

def move_left
  if @off_ground
    @action = :jump_left
    @body.apply_impulse(CP::Vec2.new(-FLY_IMPULSE, 0), CP::Vec2.new(0, 0))
  else
    @action = :run_left
    @body.apply_impulse(CP::Vec2.new(-RUN_IMPULSE, 0), CP::Vec2.new(0, 0))
  end
end
```

In the jump() method, the impulse you apply is much larger, since it will only be applied once when the spacebar is pressed, and it has to get Chip moving up to the next platform:

Escape/Escape_1/chip.rb
```
def jump
  if @off_ground
    @body.apply_impulse(CP::Vec2.new(0, -AIR_JUMP_IMPULSE),
                        CP::Vec2.new(0, 0))
  else
    @body.apply_impulse(CP::Vec2.new(0, -JUMP_IMPULSE), CP::Vec2.new(0, 0))
    if @action == :left
      @action = :jump_left
    else
      @action = :jump_right
    end
  end
end
```

The stand() method doesn't do anything to Chip but set his @action variable:

Escape/Escape_1/chip.rb
```
def stand
  @action = :stand unless off_ground
end
```

Run the game. Chip can run and jump, and he looks like he is running and jumping. To complete the game, add a mix of moving and stationary platforms so that there are a few paths Chip can follow to escape the pit.

Add Moving Platforms

Moving platforms make your game more interesting and challenging. They require the player to think ahead and try to predict where the platforms will be when Chip reaches them. Some of the platforms will move side to side, and some will move up and down.

Adding moving platforms to your physics game requires a little creativity. Platforms that move like these don't really occur in nature. You could just move them yourself by changing their position, but the result wouldn't be good. They wouldn't interact correctly with the player and the boulders. Instead, place them in the space and figure out what forces are needed to hold them up and move them back and forth. Then, you cheat the physics engine just a little to keep them where you want them.

The moving platforms will be represented by one class, MovingPlatform. A @direction variable will keep track of whether a particular platform moves up and down or side to side. Each platform will have a center position and a *range*. When the platform reaches a distance equal to the range away from the center, you start pushing it back toward the center.

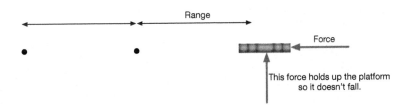

The horizontal force will push the platform to the left until it reaches the dot on the left.

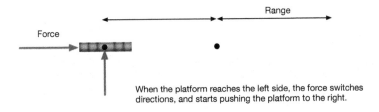

Figure 3—Moving Platforms

Push the platform all the way back through the center position until it reaches a distance from the center equal to the range on the other side. And then repeat. The platform moves back and forth, turning around at a point a little past the declared range. By adjusting constants like the range, the force, and the maximum platform velocity, you can make the platforms move the way you want.

Start by making a new file, moving_platform.rb, for the new class. Include the file in the game:

Escape/Escape_1/escape.rb
```ruby
require 'gosu'
require 'chipmunk'
require_relative 'boulder'
require_relative 'platform'
require_relative 'wall'
require_relative 'chip'
➤ require_relative 'moving_platform'
```

The initialize() method of the MovingPlatform class takes a position given by x and y, along with the direction of travel and a range as parameters. Save the x and y arguments as @x_center and @y_center. The moving platform is very heavy compared to a boulder or Chip, and it is unable to rotate. Because Chip has to jump off these platforms, give the platform @width and @height variables:

Escape/Escape_1/moving_platform.rb
```ruby
class MovingPlatform
  FRICTION = 0.7
  ELASTICITY = 0.8
  SPEED_LIMIT = 40
  attr_reader :body,:width,:height
  def initialize(window, x, y, range, direction)
    space = window.space
    @window = window
    @x_center = x
    @y_center = y
    @direction = direction
    @range = range
    @body = CP::Body.new(50000, 100.0 / 0)
    @width = 96
    @height = 16
    @body.v_limit = SPEED_LIMIT
  end
end
```

The initial position of the platform depends on whether the platform moves vertically or horizontally. By placing the platform initially at a position a little beyond its range, you ensure that it will start moving toward the center at the beginning of the game. Also create an instance variable, @move, that keeps track of which way the platform is moving:

Escape/Escape_1/moving_platform.rb

```ruby
def initialize(window, x, y, range, direction)
  space = window.space
  @window = window
  @x_center = x
  @y_center = y
  @direction = direction
  @range = range
  @body = CP::Body.new(50000, 100.0 / 0)
  @width = 96
  @height = 16
  @body.v_limit = SPEED_LIMIT
➤ if @direction == :horizontal
➤   @body.p = CP::Vec2.new(x + range + 100, y)
➤   @move = :right
➤ else
➤   @body.p = CP::Vec2.new(x, y + range + 100)
➤   @move = :down
➤ end
end
```

To finish the initialize() method of the MovingPlatform class, create the shape, which is the same as the shape of the stationary platforms. Add the body and shape to the physics space and apply an upward force to keep the moving platforms from falling to the ground:

Escape/Escape_1/moving_platform.rb

```ruby
def initialize(window, x, y, range, direction)
  space = window.space
  @window = window
  @x_center = x
  @y_center = y
  @direction = direction
  @range = range
  @body = CP::Body.new(50000, 100.0 / 0)
  @width = 96
  @height = 16
  @body.v_limit = SPEED_LIMIT
  if @direction == :horizontal
    @body.p = CP::Vec2.new(x + range + 100, y)
    @move = :right
  else
    @body.p = CP::Vec2.new(x, y + range + 100)
    @move = :down
  end
➤ bounds = [CP::Vec2.new(-48, -8),
➤          CP::Vec2.new(-48, 8),
➤          CP::Vec2.new(48, 8),
➤          CP::Vec2.new(48, -8)]
➤ shape = CP::Shape::Poly.new(@body, bounds, CP::Vec2.new(0, 0))
```

```
➤    shape.u = FRICTION
➤    shape.e = ELASTICITY
➤    space.add_body(@body)
➤    space.add_shape(shape)
➤    @image = Gosu::Image.new('images/platform.png')
➤    @body.apply_force(CP::Vec2.new(0, -20000000), CP::Vec2.new(0, 0))
    end
```

Figure 3, *Moving Platforms*, on page 147 shows the strategy you use to move the platforms. It involves pushing them in one direction with a force until the platform gets a certain distance, the range, away from its center position. Then the force switches, and the platform gets pushed the other way. Now you implement that plan as code.

There are four possibilities for the way the platform is moving. It could be moving horizontally or vertically. If it's moving horizontally, it can be moving right or left; if it's moving vertically, it can be moving up or down. Once you create and add forces to the platform, the physics engine takes care of moving it. You need to readjust the forces each time the platform moves beyond its range.

Look first at a platform moving horizontally to the right. If it has moved far enough, change its @move variable to :left. Also call the reset_forces() method, which removes all the forces on the platform. Then apply two new forces. You have to reapply the upward force that balances gravity, and apply a new force to the left. This force stops the platform over a short distance and then pushes it back to the left until it reaches the other end of the range:

Escape/Escape_1/moving_platform.rb
```
def move
  case @direction
  when :horizontal
    if @body.p.x > @x_center + @range && @move == :right
      @body.reset_forces
      @body.apply_force(CP::Vec2.new(0, -20000000), CP::Vec2.new(0, 0))
      @body.apply_force(CP::Vec2.new(-20000000, 0), CP::Vec2.new(0, 0))
      @move = :left
    end
end
```

Once it is moving left, check to see whether it has reached the other end of the range, and then adjust the forces so that it starts moving to the right. You also add one line of code to cheat the physics engine, just a little. See whether you can spot that line of code:

Escape/Escape_1/moving_platform.rb

```ruby
def move
  case @direction
  when :horizontal
    if @body.p.x > @x_center + @range && @move == :right
      @body.reset_forces
      @body.apply_force(CP::Vec2.new(0, -20000000), CP::Vec2.new(0, 0))
      @body.apply_force(CP::Vec2.new(-20000000, 0), CP::Vec2.new(0, 0))
      @move = :left
    elsif @body.p.x < @x_center - @range && @move == :left
      @body.reset_forces
      @body.apply_force(CP::Vec2.new(0, -20000000), CP::Vec2.new(0, 0))
      @body.apply_force(CP::Vec2.new(20000000, 0), CP::Vec2.new(0, 0))
      @move = :right
    end
    @body.p.y = @y_center
end
```

For an object moving left and right, you added the single line of code: @body.p.y = @y_center. This line ensures that when a boulder pushes the platform down a tiny bit, you move it back up. Without that adjustment, even though you apply a force that counteracts gravity, the platform would eventually be pushed down by the unceasing rain of boulders.

For a vertically moving platform, you do a very similar thing. When the platform is moving down, you check to see whether it has moved down far enough and start pushing it up. Only one force is applied, which is greater than the force of gravity:

Escape/Escape_1/moving_platform.rb

```ruby
def move
  case @direction
  when :horizontal
    if @body.p.x > @x_center + @range && @move == :right
      @body.reset_forces
      @body.apply_force(CP::Vec2.new(0, -20000000), CP::Vec2.new(0, 0))
      @body.apply_force(CP::Vec2.new(-20000000, 0), CP::Vec2.new(0, 0))
      @move = :left
    elsif @body.p.x < @x_center - @range && @move == :left
      @body.reset_forces
      @body.apply_force(CP::Vec2.new(0, -20000000), CP::Vec2.new(0, 0))
      @body.apply_force(CP::Vec2.new(20000000, 0), CP::Vec2.new(0, 0))
      @move = :right
    end
    @body.p.y = @y_center
  when :vertical
    if @body.p.y > @y_center + @range && @move == :down
      @body.reset_forces
      @body.apply_force(CP::Vec2.new(0, -25000000), CP::Vec2.new(0, 0))
```

```
➤        @move = :up
      end
    end
```

If the platform is moving up, you check to see when it has gone far enough and change the force so that it is less than the force of gravity, allowing the platform to start moving downward. Add a line of code to keep it horizontally in place:

Escape/Escape_1/moving_platform.rb
```
when :vertical
    if @body.p.y > @y_center + @range && @move == :down
      @body.reset_forces
      @body.apply_force(CP::Vec2.new(0, -25000000), CP::Vec2.new(0, 0))
      @move = :up
➤    elsif @body.p.y < @y_center - @range && @move == :up
➤      @body.reset_forces
➤      @body.apply_force(CP::Vec2.new(0, -15000000), CP::Vec2.new(0, 0))
➤      @move = :down
➤    end
➤    @body.p.x = @x_center
    end
```

The moving platforms need a draw() method. You get the location of the platform from the @body variable:

Escape/Escape_1/moving_platform.rb
```
def draw
    @image.draw_rot(@body.p.x, @body.p.y , 0, 1)
end
```

To give Chip a path to the top of the pit, add a mix of stationary and moving platforms. Feel free to adjust them to suit you; the ones here are just an example. In the next chapter, Chapter 9, *Making a Side-Scrolling Game*, on page 157, you'll tackle random placement of the platforms. The platforms are added to the @platforms array in the make_platforms() method, just after the four you added earlier:

Escape/Escape_1/escape.rb
```
def make_platforms
    platforms = []
    platforms.push Platform.new(self,150,700)
    platforms.push Platform.new(self,320,650)
    platforms.push Platform.new(self,150,500)
    platforms.push Platform.new(self,470,550)
➤    platforms.push MovingPlatform.new(self,580,600,70,:vertical)
➤    platforms.push Platform.new(self,320,440)
➤    platforms.push Platform.new(self,600,150)
➤    platforms.push Platform.new(self,700,450)
➤    platforms.push Platform.new(self,580,300)
```

```
➤    platforms.push MovingPlatform.new(self,190,330,50,:vertical)
➤    platforms.push MovingPlatform.new(self,450,230,70,:horizontal)
➤    platforms.push Platform.new(self,750,140)
➤    platforms.push Platform.new(self,700,700)
     return platforms
  end
```

Each time the update() method runs, you want to call the move() method on each of the moving platforms. Your @platforms array has both moving and stationary platforms, and stationary platforms don't have a move() method. In the update(), you check to see whether each platform has a move() method, and move those that do:

Escape/Escape_1/escape.rb
```
@platforms.each do |platform|
  platform.move if platform.respond_to?(:move)
end
```

Run the game now. You've got some platforms moving around and some standing still. Chip can jump between them until he gets hit by the boulders. Once you time his climb out of the pit, you'll have a game.

Time the Climb

Players will make Chip run and jump between the platforms and run off the right edge of the window near the top. You'll time how long it takes them, using the Gosu.milliseconds() method you first used way back in Whack-A-Ruby.

Write the score on the screen using an instance of Gosu::Font. In the initialize() method of the Escape class, you create this instance. Also add an image that shows the player where Chip can exit the window. The completed initialize() method, with the new code highlighted, looks like this:

Escape/Escape_1/escape.rb
```
def initialize
  super(800,800)
  self.caption = 'Escape'
  @game_over = false
  @space = CP::Space.new
  @background = Gosu::Image.new('images/background.png', tileable: true)
  @space.damping = DAMPING
  @space.gravity = CP::Vec2.new(0.0, GRAVITY)
  @boulders = []
  @platforms = make_platforms
  @floor = Wall.new(self, 400,810,800,20)
  @left_wall = Wall.new(self, -10, 400, 20,800)
  @right_wall = Wall.new(self, 810,470,20,660)
  @player = Chip.new(self,70,700)
➤ @sign = Gosu::Image.new('images/exit.png')
```

```
➤     @font = Gosu::Font.new(40)
    end
```

The game ends when Chip leaves the window. Because he can only leave above the top of the right-hand wall, you just have to check his x position. In the update() method of the Escape class, check to see whether the game is over:

Escape/Escape_1/escape.rb
```
def update
  unless @game_over
    10.times do
      @space.step(1.0/600)
    end
    if rand < BOULDER_FREQUENCY
      @boulders.push Boulder.new(self, 200 + rand(400), -20)
    end
    @player.check_footing(@platforms + @boulders)
    @platforms.each do |platform|
      platform.move if platform.respond_to?(:move)
    end
    if button_down?(Gosu::KbRight)
        @player.move_right
    elsif button_down?(Gosu::KbLeft)
      @player.move_left
    else
      @player.stand
    end
➤     if @player.x > 820
➤       @game_over = true
➤       @win_time = Gosu.milliseconds
➤     end
  end
end
```

Then, in the draw() method, you draw the exit sign. Draw the timer if the game is not over, and draw the final time if the game is over. Plus, you add the words "Game Over" in the middle of the screen—all in a lovely green font:

Escape/Escape_1/escape.rb
```
def draw
  @background.draw(0,0,0)
  @background.draw(0,529,0)
  @boulders.each do |boulder|
    boulder.draw
  end
  @platforms.each do |platform|
    platform.draw
  end
  @player.draw
```

```
➤    @sign.draw(650,30,1)
➤    if @game_over == false
➤       @seconds = (Gosu.milliseconds / 1000).to_i
➤       @font.draw("#{@seconds}", 10,20,3,1,1,0xff00ff00)
➤    else
➤       @font.draw("#{@win_time/1000}", 10,20,3,1,1,0xff00ff00)
➤       @font.draw("Game Over",200, 300, 3,2,2,0xff00ff00)
➤    end
  end
```

Time to see whether you can help Chip escape the pit. If it's too easy or too hard, you can make some changes.

Make It Your Own

In Escape, you use a physics engine to move your objects. To do this, you specify a large number of properties for each object you added to the space. Each object has a mass, rotational inertia, friction, elasticity, and maximum velocity. The physics space itself has gravity and damping properties. If you want to understand the way these properties affect the game, the best way to learn is to change them and see what happens. Make a copy of your game before you start.

Change some physics properties.

Play with some of the physics properties. See what happens if all friction is removed, or if all the elasticities are zero. See what happens when all the v_limit values are removed. When you have a feel for what they all do, try setting them to make the game as fun and challenging as you can.

Add a treasure.

Try adding a treasure, maybe on one of the platforms, that Chip has to retrieve before he can get out of the pit. You can add a third wall blocking his exit, then move it out of the way when he gets the treasure.

Add a power-up.

A power-up is an object that gives Chip a power for some amount of time. Maybe it makes him jump higher or blow past boulders. If you give Chip a huge mass, boulders will just bounce off him. You can change the mass of a body by writing something like the following:

```
@body.m = 500
```

If you increase Chip's mass by a factor of ten, you need to increase any forces you exert on him by the same factor, or he'll jump like a lead brick.

What's Next

You're not finished with Chip yet. In the next chapter, you'll make his pit deeper. Then it won't fit in the window, so you'll make the window scroll to follow Chip's movement. You'll randomize the placement of the platforms so that every game is different. And you'll add quakes to shake things up and keep those boulders moving.

CHAPTER 9

Making a Side-Scrolling Game

In the initial version of Escape, a hero named Chip jumps from platform to platform to escape a pit while boulders fall around him. It's fun, but the pit is a little small, and the game is too short. We could try making all the objects smaller so that more things fit in the window, but then it would be hard to see the action. Instead, we make the pit larger than the window, and we show just part of the pit in our window at any one time.

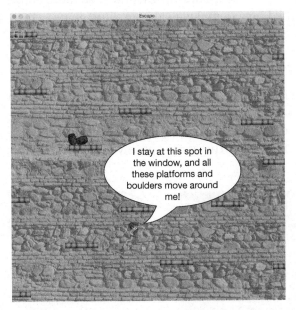

This type of game is called *side-scrolling*, because you're watching from the side as the window scrolls to follow Chip's movements. You keep the game focused on Chip and his actions by adjusting what part of the pit the player can see with an object called the *camera*.

Many games scroll the player's view in either one or both directions. It's a common technique that makes players feel as if they are moving a character or vehicle within a large world of which they see only a local piece.

In the first version of Escape, the platforms were in the same place for every game. In this version, you'll create a more random arrangement of platforms that is different each time you play.

You'll also have a little fun with the camera and introduce quakes into the game that shake the whole scene and make a bunch of boulders come down all at once. Quakes also get any boulders that have come to rest on the platforms moving again. In this chapter you'll learn to:

- Create a side-scrolling game where the game space is larger than the window.

- Generate random arrangements of platforms that are both challenging and possible for the player to beat.

- Use the camera object to add another feature—quakes—into the game.

When you're finished, your platform game will be more challenging and fun. You'll have learned how to make a side-scrolling game, which can help make your games bigger and better.

Use a Camera

In this new version of Escape, the pit is much bigger than your game window. You make the pit a square 1600 pixels on a side, while the window is 800 pixels square, so you see only one quarter of the game inside the window at any one time. The part of the game space you'll show will depend on Chip's location.

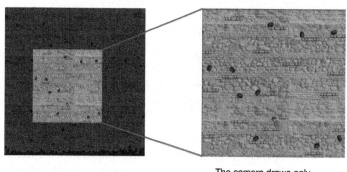

All the game objects are in
the physics space.

The camera draws only
some of the game window,
based on Chip's location.

It's as if a camera is following Chip around as he climbs out of the pit. When Chip gets close to an edge of the pit, or to the top or bottom, the camera doesn't follow him in the same way. Instead, the camera stops so that the whole camera view remains inside the pit.

The Camera Class

Start by making a copy of the Escape folder you made in the last chapter. If you don't have that, you can start with the finished project in the Escape_1 folder in the downloads for this book. You'll make only small changes to the sprite classes in the project, so keep those as part of the new game. Create a new file for your camera class called camera.rb.

Use the camera to help you draw all the objects in the pit. The camera calculates two numbers that *shift* the positions of the objects as you draw them in the window. These numbers are called x_offset and y_offset.

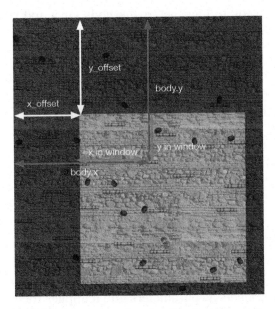

Calculating the position of an object in the window.

x = body.x - x_offset

y = body.y - y_offset

The physics space tracks the location of each object in the space, and you use that information along with the camera offsets to draw the objects in the window. The camera needs to know the sizes for the physics space and the window. In the initialize() method of Camera, you store these values and calculate the maximum offsets. You use these maximum offsets to keep the area your camera shows within the bounds of the pit when Chip is near an edge.

Escape/Escape_2/camera.rb
```ruby
class Camera
  attr_reader :x_offset,:y_offset

  def initialize(window, space_height, space_width)
    @window = window
    @space_height = space_height
    @window_height = window.height
    @space_width = space_width
    @window_width = window.width
    @x_offset_max = space_width - @window_width
    @y_offset_max = space_height - @window_height
  end
end
```

Your camera also needs a method that finds the offsets based on a sprite's location. Make that method as general as possible, because you might want to reuse your Camera class in another project. The center_on() method takes three arguments: a sprite (which needs to have getter methods for x and y) and two numbers that describe where in the window the sprite should be.

The second argument, right_margin, is the distance the sprite should be from the right edge of the window. The third, bottom_margin, is its ideal distance from the bottom. First, you calculate the offsets as shown in the preceding image. Then you make sure the camera stays within the bounds of the pit.

Escape/Escape_2/camera.rb
```ruby
def center_on(sprite, right_margin, bottom_margin)
  @x_offset = sprite.x - @window_width + right_margin
  @y_offset = sprite.y - @window_height + bottom_margin
  @x_offset = @x_offset_max if @x_offset > @x_offset_max
  @x_offset = 0 if @x_offset < 0
  @y_offset = @y_offset_max if @y_offset > @y_offset_max
  @y_offset = 0 if @y_offset < 0
end
```

To draw the images in the camera's view, you use a class method in Gosu::Window called translate(). Pass the offsets as parameters and it applies them to any drawing operations in a *block* of code. This ability to write a method that wraps a block of code is a great feature of the Ruby language, and you take advantage of it here. Add an instance method called view() to your Camera class that uses the translate() method, along with your calculated offsets.

Escape/Escape_2/camera.rb
```ruby
def view
  @window.translate(-@x_offset, -@y_offset) do
    yield
  end
end
```

The yield statement indicates that the @window.translate() method—and so also the view() method—lets you pass in a block of code. Each line in the block you supply will be executed in the *context* of the @window.translate() method. This means that any draw statements you put in the block will be translated by the camera. Which is just what you need.

Since the translate() method *adds* rather than subtracts the offsets to the position of any object drawn in its block, you send it -@x_offset and -@y_offset as parameters.

Drawing with the Camera

You draw all the objects in the pit using the camera. This means that you put their draw commands in the block of the @camera.view method. These objects include the background images, platforms, boulders, and Chip. The score is not part of the game and should stay in place in the window as Chip moves.

The initialize() method of the new Escape class is much the same as the one from the previous game. The first difference is that the walls and floor box in a space that is 1600 pixels square, which defines the size of the pit. Chip needs to be placed near the bottom of the pit, so his initial vertical position is different. Add the camera object and center the camera on Chip. Also add music so Chip has an upbeat song to help him jump. You can copy this method from the previous game and change only the highlighted lines:

Escape/Escape_2/escape2.rb
```
require 'gosu'
require 'chipmunk'
require_relative 'camera'
require_relative 'boulder'
require_relative 'platform'
require_relative 'wall'
require_relative 'chip'
require_relative 'moving_platform'

class Escape < Gosu::Window
  DAMPING = 0.90
  GRAVITY = 400.0
  BOULDER_FREQUENCY = 0.01
  attr_reader :space
  def initialize
    super(800,800)
    self.caption = 'Escape'
    @space = CP::Space.new
➤    @player = Chip.new(self, 70, 1500)
➤    @camera = Camera.new(self, 1600, 1600)
➤    @camera.center_on(@player, 400, 200)
```

```
          @game_over = false
          @background = Gosu::Image.new('images/background.png', tileable: true)
          @space.damping = DAMPING
          @space.gravity = CP::Vec2.new(0.0, GRAVITY)
          @boulders = []
          @platforms = make_platforms
➤         @floor = Wall.new(self, 800, 1610, 1600, 20)
➤         @left = Wall.new(self,-10, 800, 20, 1600)
➤         @right = Wall.new(self, 1610, 870, 20, 1460)
➤         #END_HIGHLGIHT
➤         @sign = Gosu::Image.new('images/exit.png')
➤         @font = Gosu::Font.new(40)
➤         @font_small = Gosu::Font.new(18)
➤         @music = Gosu::Song.new('sounds/zanzibar.ogg')
➤         @music.play(true)
       end
    end


    window = Escape.new
    window.show
```

In the draw() method of the Escape class, use your camera to help draw the
game. To do this, separate the objects into two groups. The first group consists
of all the objects viewed by the camera. This includes Chip, the platforms,
the boulders, and the exit sign. Moving the background image is an important
part of the illusion, so draw it with the camera also. To fill the whole pit, draw
the background image eight times, tiling it to fill the space. Include all these
drawing statements in the block you pass into @camera.view:

Escape/Escape_2/escape2.rb
```
def draw
  @camera.view do
    (0..3).each do |row|
      (0..1).each do |column|
        @background.draw(799 * column, 529 * row, 0)
      end
    end
    @sign.draw(1450, 30, 2)
    @player.draw
    @boulders.each do |boulder|
      boulder.draw
    end
    @platforms.each do |platform|
      platform.draw
    end
  end
end
```

You can also draw objects outside this method. The timer and ending messages should not move with the camera, so their draw statements are outside the @camera.view block. When the game is over, add some credits to the screen along with the "Game Over" message, using a separate method, draw_credits:

Escape/Escape_2/escape2.rb

```
def draw
  @camera.view do
    (0..3).each do |row|
      (0..1).each do |column|
        @background.draw(799 * column, 529 * row, 0)
      end
    end
    @sign.draw(1450, 30, 2)
    @player.draw
    @boulders.each do |boulder|
      boulder.draw
    end
    @platforms.each do |platform|
      platform.draw
    end
  end
➤ if @game_over == false
➤   @font.draw("#{@seconds}", 10, 20, 3, 1, 1, 0xff00ff00)
➤ else
➤   @font.draw("#{@win_time/1000}", 10, 20, 3, 1, 1, 0xff00ff00)
➤   draw_credits
➤ end
end
```

The draw_credits() method writes the credits, one line at a time, onto the screen:

Escape/Escape_2/escape2.rb

```
def draw_credits
  color = 0xff00ff00
  @font.draw('Game Over',240, 150, 3, 2, 2, color)
  @font_small.draw('Images from the SpriteLib Collection',
                    100, 300, 3, 2, 2, color)
  @font_small.draw('by WidgetWorx under the terms of the',
                    100, 350, 3, 2, 2, color)
  @font_small.draw('Common Public License.',
                    100, 400, 3, 2, 2, color)
  @font_small.draw('Music:  Zanzibar, by Kevin MacLeod',
                    100, 500, 3, 2, 2, color)
  @font_small.draw('(incompetech.com)',
                    100, 550, 3, 2, 2, color)
  @font_small.draw('Licensed under',
                    100, 600, 3, 2, 2, color)
  @font_small.draw('Creative Commons: By Attribution 3.0',
                    100, 650, 3, 2, 2, color)
```

```
@font_small.draw('http://creativecommons.org/licenses/by/3.0/',
                 100, 700, 3, 2, 2, color)
end
```

In the update() method of the Escape class, center the camera on the player. Add boulders, just as you did in the first Escape game, but now you have to spread them out over the 1600 pixels of your pit. Tell the physics space to update everything ten times. The differences from the update() method you wrote in the preceding chapter are highlighted in the following code:

Escape/Escape_2/escape2.rb
```
    def update
➤     @camera.center_on(@player, 400, 200)
      if @game_over == false
        @seconds = (Gosu.milliseconds / 1000).to_i
        10.times do
          @space.step(1.0/600)
        end
        if rand < BOULDER_FREQUENCY
➤         @boulders.push Boulder.new(self, 200 + rand(1200), -20)
        end
➤       if @player.x > 1620
          @game_over = true
          @win_time = Gosu.milliseconds
        end
        @player.check_footing(@platforms + @boulders)
        if button_down?(Gosu::KbRight)
          @player.move_right
        elsif button_down?(Gosu::KbLeft)
          @player.move_left
        else
          @player.stand
        end
        @platforms.each do |platform|
          platform.move if platform.respond_to?(:move)
        end
      end
    end
```

The button_down(id) method is the same as the one in the previous chapter:

Escape/Escape_2/escape2.rb
```
def button_down(id)
  if id == Gosu::KbSpace
    @player.jump
  end
  if id == Gosu::KbQ
    close
  end
end
```

Before the game will run, you need to add a make_platforms() method that returns an array of platforms. In the next section, you'll focus on this method, creating a random arrangement of moving and stationary platforms so that each game Chip needs to follow a different path out of the pit. For now, so you can test what you've written so far, you can just add a method that returns an empty array:

Escape/Escape_2/escape2.rb

```
def make_platforms
  platforms = []
  return platforms
end
```

When you run the game now, boulders fall from above, and Chip can run across the floor. When he runs far enough to the right, the camera starts to follow him. When he approaches the right-hand side of the pit, the camera reaches its maximum offset_x and stops moving. Chip can jump, but without platforms he won't get very far.

Place Platforms Randomly

In the first version of Escape, we placed the platforms ourselves, by specifying the position of each one. This meant every time someone played the game, the platforms were in the same spots. This is not necessarily a bad thing, because you can design the pit to be just as difficult as you like. In this version, try another strategy and place the platforms randomly. The three pictures that follow do not show the actual placement of platforms in the game. They help explain what you are doing in the calculations that actually place the platforms.

To place the platforms randomly, while still making the game playable each time, start by placing the platforms in a rectangular grid. The picture shows a region of the pit with the platforms placed this way.

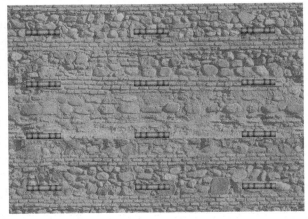

Then every other row is shifted left, so that the platforms are in a pattern that is much easier for Chip to navigate.

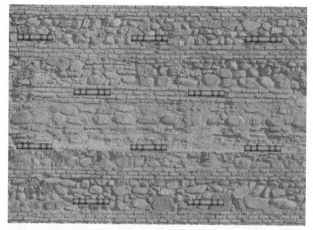

Each platform is moved by a random amount in the horizontal direction and a random amount in the vertical direction. This jumbles them up nicely and makes certain paths much easier than others.

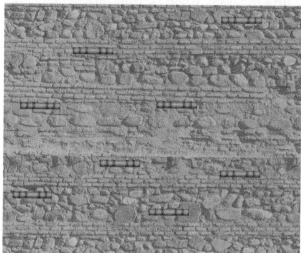

Finally, some of the platforms are made into moving platforms, and some are taken away entirely, leaving empty spaces that Chip will have to work around. The distribution of platforms is as follows:

- 50 percent of the platforms are stationary.

- 20 percent of the platforms move vertically.

- 20 percent of the platforms move horizontally.

- 10 percent of the platforms are removed.

These numbers are all easy to adjust if you find the game too easy or too hard. You also add one nonrandom platform near the escape sign to help Chip run out of the pit.

In the make_platforms() method, you implement this strategy. Make a double loop with eleven rows and five columns. The position of each platform in the rectangular grid is calculated based on its row and column. If its row is even, slide it to the left by 150 pixels. Then its position is changed by a random number. Finally, choose a random number to decide whether the platform is stationary or moving. The moving ones have a 50 percent chance each of moving horizontally or vertically. If the random number num is greater than 0.9, no platform is added at all:

Escape/Escape_2/escape2.rb

```
def make_platforms
  platforms = []
  (0..10).each do |row|
    (0..4).each do |column|
      x = column * 300 + 200
      y = row * 140 + 100
      if row % 2 == 0
        x -= 150
      end
      x += rand(100) - 50
      y += rand(100) - 50
      num = rand
      if num < 0.40
        direction = rand < 0.5 ? :vertical : :horizontal
        range = 30 + rand(40)
        platforms.push MovingPlatform.new(self, x,y,range, direction)
      elsif num < 0.90
        platforms.push Platform.new(self,x,y)
      end
    end
  end
  platforms.push Platform.new(self,1550,140)
  return platforms
end
```

When you play now, each arrangement of platforms is different. Try getting to the top. It's pretty challenging, especially since you can't see the platforms that are outside of the window. You could stop now, but before you do, use the camera object to add one more feature to the game.

Shake Your Camera

You added the camera to the game so that you can follow Chip as he leaps his way out of the pit. By moving the camera, you show a region of the pit in Chip's vicinity. In this section, you'll take advantage of the camera and add a new feature to the game. Quakes happen randomly. When a quake occurs, the pit appears to shake, and a bunch of boulders rain down all at once. If

Chip is near the top during a quake, he'd better move quickly to avoid the boulders. You don't actually move Chip, the pit, or the platforms during a quake; you just shake the camera, and it looks like everything is shaking. At the same time, give each of the boulders already in the game a random shove, adding to the illusion.

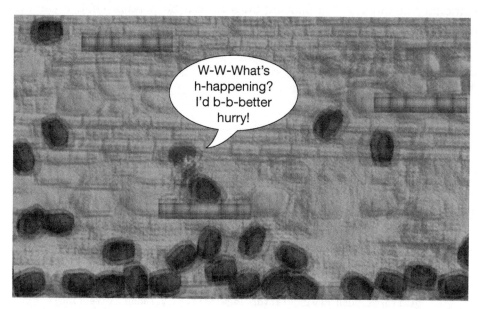

Each quake lasts 30 frames, which is half a second, and each frame of the quake you offset the camera a little bit both vertically and horizontally. You use a strategy similar to the one you used to make the ruby image appear for a short time in Whack-A-Ruby. You create a variable @quake_time, which is the number of frames left in a quake. In the initialize() method of the Escape class, you set that variable to 0 and also add a sound effect for the quakes:

Escape/Escape_2/escape2.rb
```
def initialize
  super(800,800)
  self.caption = 'Escape'
  @space = CP::Space.new
➤ @player = Chip.new(self, 70, 1500)
➤ @camera = Camera.new(self, 1600, 1600)
➤ @camera.center_on(@player, 400, 200)
  @game_over = false
  @background = Gosu::Image.new('images/background.png', tileable: true)
  @space.damping = DAMPING
  @space.gravity = CP::Vec2.new(0.0, GRAVITY)
  @boulders = []
  @platforms = make_platforms
➤ @floor = Wall.new(self, 800, 1610, 1600, 20)
```

```
➤    @left = Wall.new(self,-10, 800, 20, 1600)
➤    @right = Wall.new(self, 1610, 870, 20, 1460)
➤    #END_HIGHLGIHT
➤    @sign = Gosu::Image.new('images/exit.png')
➤    @font = Gosu::Font.new(40)
➤    @font_small = Gosu::Font.new(18)
➤    @music = Gosu::Song.new('sounds/zanzibar.ogg')
➤    @music.play(true)
➤    @quake_time = 0
➤    @quake_sound = Gosu::Sample.new('sounds/quake.ogg')
    end
```

Make a method called quake() in the Escape class that starts a quake. This
method sets the quake_time variable and plays the quake sound. It also sends
each boulder a push:

Escape/Escape_2/escape2.rb
```
def quake
  @quake_time = 30
  @quake_sound.play
  @boulders.each do |boulder|
    boulder.quake
  end
end
```

Then you write the quake() method for the Boulder class. In it, give each boulder
the same shove that you gave it when it was created. It's enough to get many
of the boulders that have come to rest on platforms moving again:

Escape/Escape_2/boulder.rb
```
def quake
    @body.apply_impulse(CP::Vec2.new(rand(100000) - 50000, 100000),
                               CP::Vec2.new(rand*0.8 - 0.4, 0))
end
```

In the update() method of the Escape class, decrement the @quake_time variable.
If @quake_time is still greater than 0, you're still quaking, so shake the camera.
You also create a new boulder *much* more frequently than when there is no
quake. Because a quake lasts 30 frames, and you have a one-fifth chance
per frame of creating a boulder, each quake creates an average of six boulders:

Escape/Escape_2/escape2.rb
```
def update
  @camera.center_on(@player, 400, 200)
  if @game_over == false
    @seconds = (Gosu.milliseconds / 1000).to_i
    10.times do
      @space.step(1.0/600)
    end
    if rand < BOULDER_FREQUENCY
```

```
        @boulders.push Boulder.new(self, 200 + rand(1200), -20)
      end
      if @player.x > 1620
        @game_over = true
        @win_time = Gosu.milliseconds
      end
      @player.check_footing(@platforms + @boulders)
      if button_down?(Gosu::KbRight)
          @player.move_right
      elsif button_down?(Gosu::KbLeft)
        @player.move_left
      else
        @player.stand
      end
      @platforms.each do |platform|
        platform.move if platform.respond_to?(:move)
      end
➤     if rand < 0.001
➤       quake
➤     end
➤     @quake_time -= 1
➤     if @quake_time > 0
➤       @camera.shake
➤       if rand < 0.2
➤         @boulders.push Boulder.new(self, 200 + rand(1200), -20)
➤       end
➤     end
➤   end
➤ end
```

Finally, you write the shake() method of the Camera class. Note that you read just the camera to Chip's position each frame, so you don't need to *unshake* the camera; that already happens automatically:

Escape/Escape_2/camera.rb
```
def shake
  @x_offset += rand(9) - 4
  @y_offset += rand(9) - 4
end
```

Now you've got quakes! Play the game and see how quickly you can reach the exit.

Make It Your Own

Making Escape added a few tools to your kit. You learned to make a game using the Chipmunk physics engine, and you learned how to make a side-scrolling platformer. As in your other games, there are plenty of things for you to change. Anywhere you added a random chance, distance, or time is an opportunity for you to experiment and tweak the game to your liking. You can make bigger changes, too, by adding new features to the game. Make a copy before you begin.

Have fun with the camera.

What else can you do with the camera object? The rules for the camera are pretty simple. Try having the camera adjust to give the player a longer view in the direction Chip is moving. Give the camera a maximum velocity so that it can't move as fast as Chip.

Add more objects.

Put stars on each platform that you have to gather before the gate opens. Add exploding boulders that give Chip a huge shove when they explode. Add a creature that blinks between platforms and that you can't pass. Add platforms that move in circles. Add a glowing arrow that points toward the location of the exit.

Learn more of Chipmunk.

In making Escape, you explored only part of what the Chipmunk physics engine can do. Reading the Chipmunk documentation[1] may give you some ideas. There are many aspects of Chipmunk you didn't touch on in Escape. Constraints in particular are a rich topic to explore. Maybe you'll get a great idea for your next game just by learning more of Chipmunk's capabilities.

What's Next

If you've worked through the whole book to this point, you've created four games using Ruby and Gosu. You've adjusted them to suit your needs, and hopefully you've completed some challenges to make them better. To let your friends play these games on their computers, you'll need to send them a copy of your game they can run. In the next and final chapter of this book, you'll learn to *package* your games, making Windows or OS X executables that can be easily shared.

---

1. http://beoran.github.io/chipmunk/

CHAPTER 10

Package and Share Your Game

You've finished your game. It's fun and just the right difficulty. At least, *you* think it is. Now it's time to share it with your friends and see what they think. It's also time to see whether they can beat your high score. Feedback from other players is the best way to get better. Your friends can tell you what works and what doesn't, and what's fun and what's not so great.

You can already play the game, but it's a folder full of files, and you can only run it because you set up a development environment with Ruby and Gosu, back in Chapter 2, *Get Ready*, on page 5. You don't want to make your friends set up their computers the same way—you just want to send them the game and let them play. Next, you'll learn how to turn that folder full of files into an application that anyone can use.

In this chapter, as an example, you'll package up the Sector Five game you finished in Chapter 6, *Adding Scenes and Sounds*, on page 79, but the procedure you follow will work for any game you make. This process of *packaging* a game is completely different for Windows and Mac OS X applications. If you're packaging for Windows, read on. If you're packaging for OS X, skip ahead to *Packaging for OS X*, on page 175.

Packaging for Windows

You package your game using the same command-line tool you used in Chapter 2, *Get Ready*, on page 5. You get a new Ruby gem, called ocra, which you use to create your executable.

Run the Command Prompt application. At the prompt, type the first line of the following:

```
C:\ gem install ocra
Fetching: ocra-1.3.5.gem (100%)
Successfully installed ocra-1.3.5
```

To use ocra, you need to first use cd to move into the directory where your game files are. In this tutorial, the SectorFive folder is on the desktop, so at the command line you can type the following command.

```
C:\Users\mark> cd Desktop/SectorFive
C:\Users\mark\Desktop\SectorFive>
```

The ocra command needs to be followed with the name of the main Ruby file in your game, and then with a list of the resources you want included in the packaged application. The --chdir-first option tells ocra where to look for the image and other resources. List all the pictures, sounds, and any other files you've used, or if they are in folders, simply list the folders. It's easy to include extra images and sounds that you're not using this way, so move out any files you don't need before you start. Your gems, such as Gosu and Chipmunk, and any Ruby files you've required will be included automatically. You can choose the name of the executable with the --output flag. To package SectorFive, type the first line shown in the following session. The game will actually run, as ocra figures out all the files it needs to include. You can play or just quit, and ocra will finish, providing many lines of output:

```
C:\SectorFive>ocra --chdir-first --output SectorFive.exe \
sector_five_scenes.rb images sounds credits.txt

=== Loading script to check dependencies
=== Detected gem ocra-1.3.5 (loaded, files)
===    6 files, 19031 bytes
=== Detected gem gosu-0.9.2-x86-mingw32 (loaded, files)
===    38 files, 9283787 bytes
=== Including 52 encoding support files (2836480 bytes, use --
    no-enc to exclude)
=== Building SectorFive
=== Adding user-supplied source files
=== Adding ruby executable ruby.exe

... more ...

=== Adding library files
=== Compressing  52191268 bytes
=== Finished building SectorFive (33786909 bytes)
```

Running this script will take a while. When it's finished, a new file will be created, SectorFive.exe. This is the executable file that you can share with your friends. It contains your game, along with Ruby, Gosu, and all the media files included in your game. You might notice that SectorFive.exe is a 34MB file, which is pretty big! We'll discuss how you can share it in *Share Your Game*, on page 178.

Packaging for OS X

To package the game, you download a *wrapper* from the Gosu website. This is a complete application, written with Ruby and Gosu. It doesn't do much, but has the whole environment needed to run the game. Then you'll replace the application inside the wrapper with your game. Finally, you'll make a few changes to a file called Info.plist. Then you can share it with your friends.

Get the Wrapper Application

The authors of Gosu have provided an application wrapper so you can make an OS X app from your Ruby/Gosu game. Using your browser, go to https://github.com/gosu/ruby_app/releases/.

From that site, download the latest Ruby.app.zip. Find it in your downloads, unzip the file, and move it to your desktop. When you run the app, you'll probably see a message like this one.

This message appears because Apple is protecting you from malware. In System Preferences, open the Security and Privacy panel.

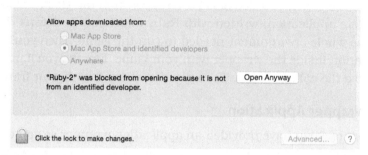

The default settings are to only run applications from the Mac App Store and identified developers. You could change your settings to run applications from anywhere, but a safer choice is to choose Open Anyway to allow just this one to run, while leaving the default protection in place. *When you distribute your game, your users will likely get the same message and will need to take the same steps to fix it.*

When you finally run the Ruby.app application, a big ruby rocks gently back and forth in a window on your screen. The next step is to replace that ruby with your game.

Open the Wrapper

An application on OS X is really a folder. Double-clicking a normal folder opens the folder and lets you see what is inside, but double-clicking Ruby.app runs the application. To see inside it, right-click (or hold down the Control key while you click) on the Ruby.app icon in the Finder.

From the contextual menu, choose Show Package Contents. Here is a column view from the Finder, showing what is inside the Ruby.app file before you make your changes.

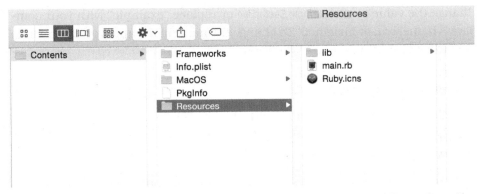

The application package always runs the file named main.rb. To replace the sample app with your game, first remove main.rb and move your whole game —ruby files, pictures, sounds, and all—into its place. Make sure you *don't* remove the lib folder—that's where Gosu and a whole bunch of other files are. Then rename the game file—in this case, sector_five_scenes.rb—to main.rb. Here is the same file structure with your game in place.

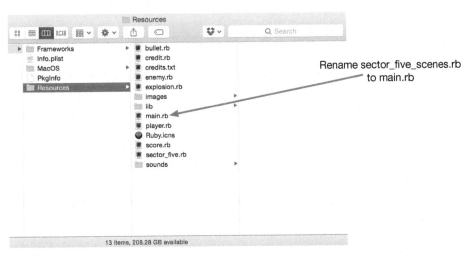

Then you make some changes to a file called Info.plist. This file, according to Apple's developer website, is "a structured text file that contains essential configuration information for a bundled executable." And since you're turning your game into a bundled executable, you put some information about your game into the Info.plist file. Start by opening Info.plist in your text editor.

The Info.plist file is a list of *keys* and values. For instance, in the following section, the key CFBundleIdentifier is associated with the value com.example.Ruby:

```
<key>CFBundleIdentifier</key>
<string>com.example.Ruby</string>
```

Change the value to com.example.SectorFive or replace "example" with your company's name, real or imagined. To change the name of the app, you can include a new key and value:

```
<key>CFBundleDisplayName</key>
<string>Sector Five</string>
```

Also change the value associated with the key CFName:

```
<key>CFBundleName</key>
<string>Sector Five</string>
```

After you make these changes to Info.plist, you can change the name of your application package directory to Sector Five in the Finder. If you change the name without changing Info.plist first, your application will become broken and you won't be able to run it.

Before you share your OS X game, you should compress it into a zip file. Right-click (or Control-click) on the file and choose Compress SectorFive from the contextual menu. You can share the resulting zip file over email or a file-sharing service.

Share Your Game

Now you have a game that you're ready to share. The applications you've created are pretty large files. For SectorFive, the Windows executable is about 40MB, and the compressed OS X app bundle is 32MB. This is because each package includes a complete Ruby and Gosu installation, as well as any system resources that might be needed. To make sure the game runs on a wide range of computers, a lot of things are included. For this reason, you might want to share your game with a file-sharing service, such as Dropbox or Google Drive, rather than using email. Some email services, including Gmail, have file-size limits for attachments.

What's Next

We've made some games together. You've tried some challenges and made some changes of your own to the games you've made. It's time for you to make your own games. Maybe one of the games in this book gave you an idea for a new game, or maybe a game you played on your phone will get your juices flowing. Make some games and share them. If you make one you're proud of, I hope you'll let me know and send me a copy.

One next step you can take, after sharing your games, is sharing your code. Get some friends interested and swap games and ideas. Work on a game together. If you're in school, start a club or other organization to promote game programming.

Many metropolitan areas have Ruby user groups that meet periodically. The people at those groups might be working on things other than games, but they are all interested in Ruby, and many will likely be interested in helping Ruby programmers grow their skills. And, just like you, many programmers got started by writing games, and they still may find game writing hard to resist.

Thanks again for reading this book. I trust you've learned something about writing games and that your programming skills have grown. It's time to say goodbye and leave you to write some games yourself. Good luck, and happy game-writing!

Resources

Documentation

The Gosu gem has a great Ruby documentation site, with a list of every class and method with many examples. You can find it at http://www.libgosu.org/rdoc/. On that page, look for the tabs at the top right to find the documentation.

The Chipmunk gem has some great documentation as well. You can find it at http://beoran.github.io/chipmunk/.

Images and Sounds

There are some great resources online that provide free graphics to aspiring game writers. A few are listed here to get you started, and you can find many more by searching. Pay attention to the licenses under which art and music are released, and give credit to the artists as appropriate.

OpenGameArt.org
> This is has a tremendous amount of free art and has some good search tools as well. You can search by keyword, by type of art, or by license. Some sound effects are on this site as well. http://www.opengameart.org

Incompetech.com
> Incompetech is a website where Kevin MacLeod shares and sells his musical creations. He has created a wide range of music that you can search by type and mood. Some of the background music in Sector Five came from this site. http://www.incompetech.com

Wikimedia Commons
> You can find this site at http://commons.wikimedia.org. It is a collection of more than 24 million freely usable photographs. The background image in Escape is from this site.

OpenClipArt

Lots of free clip art at http://www.openclipart.org. The images of the ruby and hammer in Whack-A-Ruby are from this site.

Clker.com

A site of free clip art at http://www.clker.com. The exit sign in Escape is from this site.

WidgetWorx.com

WidgetWorx is the creation of Ari Feldman and features SpriteLib, a collection of free sprites. The sprites in Escape—including the hero, Chip—are from this collection. http://www.widgetworx.com

Bibliography

[FH13]   Dave Thomas, with Chad Fowler and Andy Hunt. *Programming Ruby 1.9 & 2.0 (4th edition)*. The Pragmatic Bookshelf, Raleigh, NC, and Dallas, TX, 4th, 2013.

[Pin09]   Chris Pine. *Learn to Program (2nd edition)*. The Pragmatic Bookshelf, Raleigh, NC, and Dallas, TX, 2nd, 2009.

Index

Get Kids into Programming

Get your kids writing Minecraft plugins in Java, or 3D games in JavaScript. No experience required!

Learn to Program with Minecraft Plugins (2nd edition)

The bestselling, kid-tested book for Minecraft is now updated for CanaryMod! Write your own Minecraft plugins and watch your code come to life with flaming cows, flying creepers, teleportation, and interactivity. Add your own features to the Minecraft game by developing Java code that "plugs in" to the server. You'll manipulate and control elements in the 3D graphical game environment without having to write tons of code or learn huge frameworks. No previous programming experience necessary.

Andy Hunt
(284 pages) ISBN: 9781941222942. $29
https://pragprog.com/book/ahmine2

3D Game Programming for Kids

You know what's even better than playing games? Creating your own. Even if you're an absolute beginner, this book will teach you how to make your own online games with interactive examples. You'll learn programming using nothing more than a browser, and see cool, 3D results as you type. You'll learn real-world programming skills in a real programming language: JavaScript, the language of the web. You'll be amazed at what you can do as you build interactive worlds and fun games. Appropriate for ages 10-99!

Printed in full color.

Chris Strom
(308 pages) ISBN: 9781937785444. $36
https://pragprog.com/book/csjava

Tinker, Tailor, Solder, and DIY!

Get into the DIY spirit with Raspberry Pi or Arduino. What will you build next?

Raspberry Pi: A Quick-Start Guide (2nd edition)

The Raspberry Pi is one of the most successful open source hardware projects ever. For less than $40, you get a full-blown PC, a multimedia center, and a web server—and this book gives you everything you need to get started. You'll learn the basics, progress to controlling the Pi, and then build your own electronics projects. This new edition is revised and updated with two new chapters on adding digital and analog sensors, and creating videos and a burglar alarm with the Pi camera. *Printed in full color.*

Maik Schmidt
(176 pages) ISBN: 9781937785802. $22
https://pragprog.com/book/msraspi2

Arduino: A Quick-Start Guide, Second Edition

Arduino is an open-source platform that makes DIY electronics projects easier than ever. Gone are the days when you had to learn electronics theory and arcane programming languages before you could even get an LED to blink. Now, with this new edition of the best-selling *Arduino: A Quick-Start Guide*, readers with no electronics experience can create their first gadgets quickly. This book is up-to-date for the latest Arduino boards and for Arduino 1.x, with step-by-step instructions for building a universal remote, a motion-sensing game controller, and many other fun, useful projects.

Maik Schmidt
(324 pages) ISBN: 9781941222249. $34
https://pragprog.com/book/msard2

Sound and Android

Add live sound to your apps, or create your own scripts on Android.

Programming Sound with Pure Data

Sound gives your native, web, or mobile apps that extra dimension, and it's essential for games. Rather than using canned samples from a sample library, learn how to build sounds from the ground up and produce them for web projects using the Pure Data programming language. Even better, you'll be able to integrate dynamic sound environments into your native apps or games—sound that reacts to the app, instead of sounding the same every time. Start your journey as a sound designer, and get the power to craft the sound you put into your digital experiences.

Tony Hillerson
(196 pages) ISBN: 9781937785666. $36
https://pragprog.com/book/thsound

Developing Android on Android

Take advantage of the open, tinker-friendly Android platform and make your device work the way you want it to. Quickly create Android tasks, scripts, and programs entirely on your Android device—no PC required. Learn how to build your own innovative Android programs and workflows with tools you can run on Android itself, and tailor the Android default user interface to match your mobile lifestyle needs. Apply your favorite scripting language to rapidly develop programs that speak the time and battery level, alert you to important events or locations, read your new email to you, and much more.

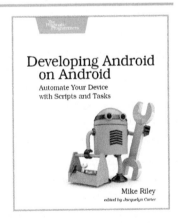

Mike Riley
(232 pages) ISBN: 9781937785543. $36
https://pragprog.com/book/mrand

The Joy of Mazes and Math

Rediscover the joy and fascinating weirdness of mazes and pure mathematics.

Mazes for Programmers

A book on mazes? Seriously?

Yes!

Not because you spend your day creating mazes, or because you particularly like solving mazes.

But because it's fun. Remember when programming used to be fun? This book takes you back to those days when you were starting to program, and you wanted to make your code do things, draw things, and solve puzzles. It's fun because it lets you explore and grow your code, and reminds you how it feels to just think.

Sometimes it feels like you live your life in a maze of twisty little passages, all alike. Now you can code your way out.

Jamis Buck
(286 pages) ISBN: 9781680500554. $38
https://pragprog.com/book/jbmaze

Good Math

Mathematics is beautiful—and it can be fun and exciting as well as practical. *Good Math* is your guide to some of the most intriguing topics from two thousand years of mathematics: from Egyptian fractions to Turing machines; from the real meaning of numbers to proof trees, group symmetry, and mechanical computation. If you've ever wondered what lay beyond the proofs you struggled to complete in high school geometry, or what limits the capabilities of the computer on your desk, this is the book for you.

Mark C. Chu-Carroll
(282 pages) ISBN: 9781937785338. $34
https://pragprog.com/book/mcmath

The Modern Web

Get up to speed on the latest HTML, CSS, and JavaScript techniques.

HTML5 and CSS3 (2nd edition)

HTML5 and CSS3 are more than just buzzwords—they're the foundation for today's web applications. This book gets you up to speed on the HTML5 elements and CSS3 features you can use right now in your current projects, with backwards compatible solutions that ensure that you don't leave users of older browsers behind. This new edition covers even more new features, including CSS animations, IndexedDB, and client-side validations.

Brian P. Hogan
(314 pages) ISBN: 9781937785598. $38
https://pragprog.com/book/bhh52e

Async JavaScript

With the advent of HTML5, front-end MVC, and Node.js, JavaScript is ubiquitous—and still messy. This book will give you a solid foundation for managing async tasks without losing your sanity in a tangle of callbacks. It's a fast-paced guide to the most essential techniques for dealing with async behavior, including PubSub, evented models, and Promises. With these tricks up your sleeve, you'll be better prepared to manage the complexity of large web apps and deliver responsive code.

Trevor Burnham
(104 pages) ISBN: 9781937785277. $17
https://pragprog.com/book/tbajs

The Pragmatic Bookshelf

The Pragmatic Bookshelf features books written by developers for developers. The titles continue the well-known Pragmatic Programmer style and continue to garner awards and rave reviews. As development gets more and more difficult, the Pragmatic Programmers will be there with more titles and products to help you stay on top of your game.

Visit Us Online

This Book's Home Page
https://pragprog.com/book/msgpkids
Source code from this book, errata, and other resources. Come give us feedback, too!

Register for Updates
https://pragprog.com/updates
Be notified when updates and new books become available.

Join the Community
https://pragprog.com/community
Read our weblogs, join our online discussions, participate in our mailing list, interact with our wiki, and benefit from the experience of other Pragmatic Programmers.

New and Noteworthy
https://pragprog.com/news
Check out the latest pragmatic developments, new titles and other offerings.

Save on the eBook

Save on the eBook versions of this title. Owning the paper version of this book entitles you to purchase the electronic versions at a terrific discount.

PDFs are great for carrying around on your laptop—they are hyperlinked, have color, and are fully searchable. Most titles are also available for the iPhone and iPod touch, Amazon Kindle, and other popular e-book readers.

Buy now at *https://pragprog.com/coupon*

Contact Us

Online Orders:	*https://pragprog.com/catalog*
Customer Service:	*support@pragprog.com*
International Rights:	*translations@pragprog.com*
Academic Use:	*academic@pragprog.com*
Write for Us:	*http://write-for-us.pragprog.com*
Or Call:	+1 800-699-7764

CPSIA information can be obtained
at www.ICGtesting.com
Printed in the USA
BVOW07s1044200416

444944BV00001B/14/P